the GUITAR GRIMOIRE®

BY ADAM KADMON

the FINGERPICKING BOOK

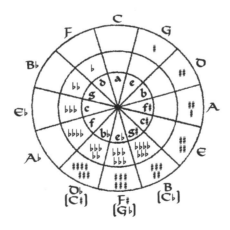

Produced by

⭐®METATRON INC.

for

CARL FISCHER®

65 Bleecker Street, New York, NY 10012

GT103

ISBN 0-8258-3926-2

For more information on **The Guitar Grimoire**® Series and other music instructional products by Adam Kadmon check out the following websites:

http://www.guitargrimoire.com

http://www.adamkadmon.com

CONTENTS

CONTENTS CONTINUED

PART ONE

CHORD FINGERPICKING

FINGERPICKING

We all dig really hot electric guitar, well most of us do. But there is something cool when a really hot electric guitarist pulls out an acoustic guitar and starts fingerpicking some really nice stuff, not just strumming some chords with a pick but fingerpicking. Going beyond that it is cool seeing electric guitarists who don't even use a pick, just fingers. Well you are going to learn how to fingerpick.

The chord examples for each of the eight chord fingerpicking patterns are more than adequate to understand the idea. The examples of chord fingerpicking patterns are given with the most frequently used major and minor open and bar chords. All the examples are working and functional, in other words, you can start applying them now over progressions as you create your own songs. Once you learn these you'll be able to apply them to any chord voicings. You will also then be able to create your own variations. The scale exercises are the most important ones. And you will be using them for the rest of your life.

It is assumed that you know how to hold a guitar and play a few chords as this is not for the total absolute beginner. But for the sake of those who know some chords but don't know anything about reading music, we are going to cover the basics of notation.

UNDERSTANDING THE NOTES

In order to understand written music or notation you have to memorize the lines and spaces of the staff, those are the five lines that the notes are written on. You also have to know the extra little lines above and below the staff which are called ledger lines.

There is an easy way to memorize the lines and spaces. The trick is to make phrases using the pitch letter as the first letter of a word. For instance, the lines of the treble clef can be the phrase, "EVERY GOOD BOY DOES FINE". The lines of the bass clef can be the phrase, "GREAT BIG DOGS FIGHT ANIMALS". The spaces of the treble clef spell the word FACE, while the spaces of the bass clef make up the phrase of "ALL CARS EAT GAS".

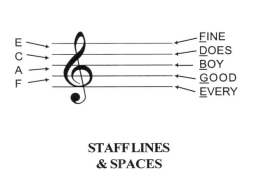

STAFF LINES & SPACES

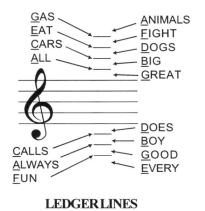

LEDGER LINES & SPACES

When we want to alter the pitch we use flat & sharp symbols on the line or space in front of the note.

SHARPS & FLATS

3

MIDDLE C AND GUITAR NOTATION

Music for guitar is written an octave higher than the piano, even though it is written with the treble clef.

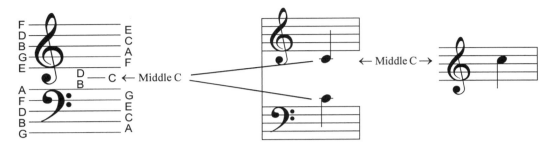

To understand the reason for this let's go back to the notes used to tune the guitar.

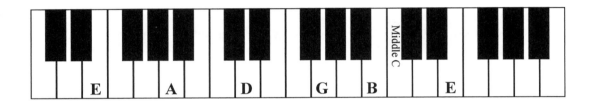

The notes for the six strings of the guitar in piano notation look like this.

If we write the notes on the treble clef without raising them an octave all the notes are on ledger lines below the staff. This can become tedious and cumbersome.

By writing the notes an octave higher, we take away much of the confusion that excessive ledger lines produce.

RHYTHM AND TIME SIGNATURES

The staves and ledger lines are then divided up into measures so that we can write music on them.

At the beginning of a song following the clef is the time signature. The top number tells how many beats the measure gets and the bottom number tells what type of note receives the beat. Often, $\frac{4}{4}$ time is written as ¢, which stands for common time and means the same thing.

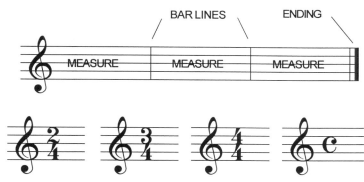

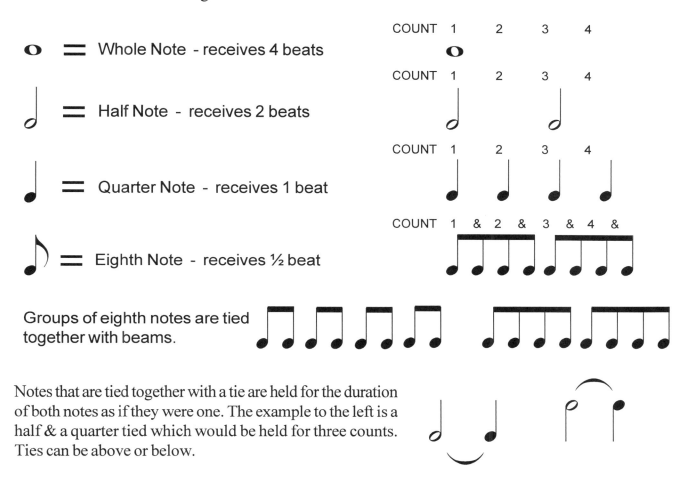

○ ═ Whole Note - receives 4 beats

𝅗𝅥 ═ Half Note - receives 2 beats

♩ ═ Quarter Note - receives 1 beat

♪ ═ Eighth Note - receives ½ beat

Groups of eighth notes are tied together with beams.

Notes that are tied together with a tie are held for the duration of both notes as if they were one. The example to the left is a half & a quarter tied which would be held for three counts. Ties can be above or below.

When we have silence in music this is what we call rests. There are various types of rests with time values just like the notes.

WHOLE REST   HALF REST   QUARTER REST   EIGHTH REST

TABLATURE

As a system of musical notation various forms of tablature have been in use for centuries. During the European Renaissance and Baroque periods tab diagrams were common for many string instruments including the lute and early guitar. In modern guitar tablature a six line staff literally represents the fingerboard; each line indicating a specific string (fig. 1).

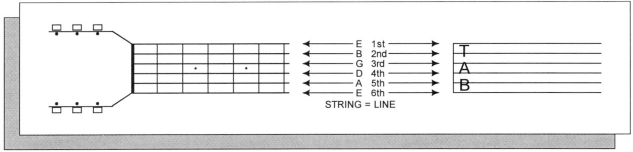

fig. 1

A number placed on a line indicates the fret number on which the string is to be played (an "O" indicates an open string) (fig. 2).

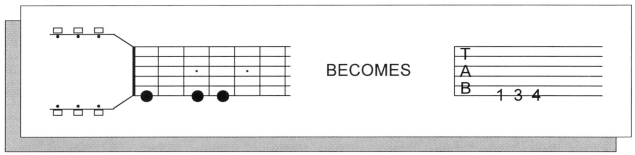

fig. 2

In tablature form a standard chord diagram looks like the example in figure 3 below.

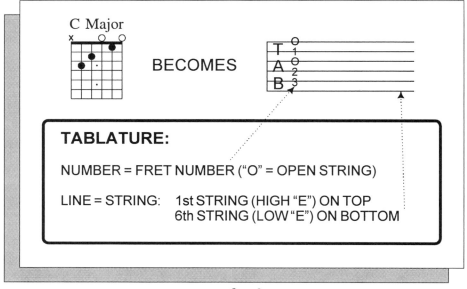

fig. 3

6

FINGERING

When fingerpicking, you have to deal with right hand fingering as well as left hand fingering. The thumb for keyboard students is considered finger number 1 which, personally, makes more sense. For the guitar, however, the left hand is T for thumb, 1 for the index finger, 2 for the middle finger, 3 for the ring finger, and 4 for the pinky.

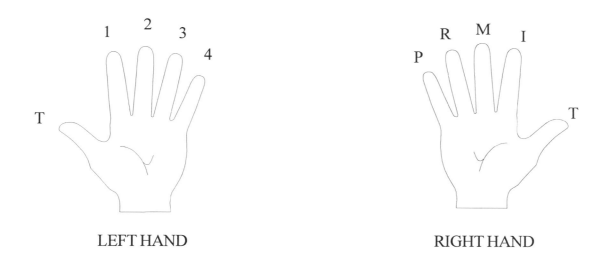

LEFT HAND   RIGHT HAND

The right hand changes a little. The thumb is T, but now the fingers are designated by a I for index finger, M for middle finger, R for ring finger, and P for pinky. Since all the guitar books have been written in this ridiculous format for decades we'll do the same so as not to confuse anyone.

In the chord section each figerpicking pattern is laid out with the familiar chord diagram to the left. The chord diagram has the left hand fingering. Above the diagram are the open or deadened strings, and below are the numeric or intervallic formulas.

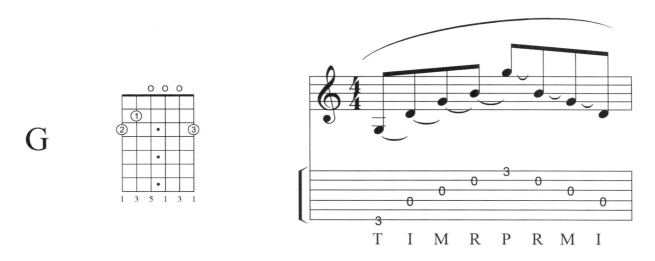

To the right is the notation and TAB. Beneath the TAB is the right hand fingerpicking pattern.

PATTERN 1

The first pattern is a simple one. Think of it as a T, I, M, R, P, R, M, I pattern which represents the fingers used in playing this pattern. This pattern is used on chord voicings that utilize five strings. I have given you a few examples of this pattern with simple major and minor chords, but you can use any chord. Once you get the hang of this pattern on these chords it will be a snap applying them to any chord.

The notes are eighth notes, but keep in mind that they keep sustaining while you are picking the other notes. That is the reason for all the ties and slurs.

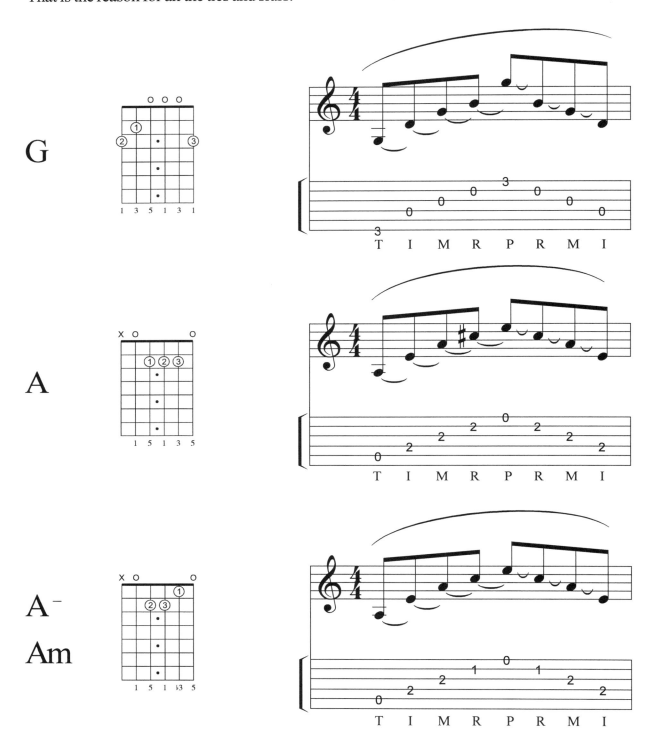

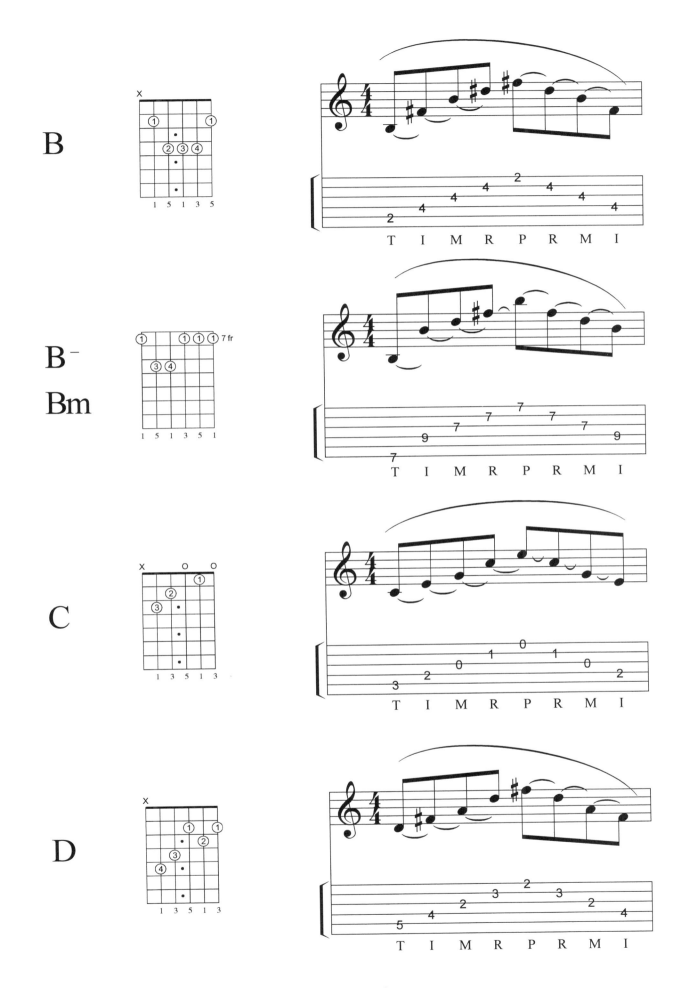

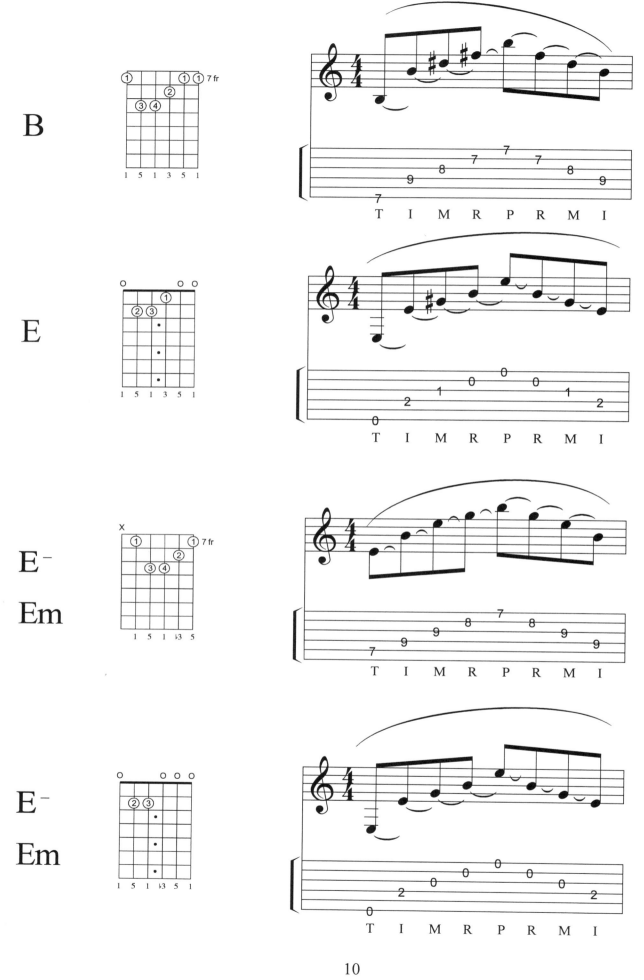

PATTERN 2

The next pattern is a T, I, M, R pattern. This is a pattern that covers four strings. Chords that use five or six strings can be fingerpicked in different ways. This is demonstrated below with the G chord. Once you understand the principle it can be applied to all the other chords in the same way.

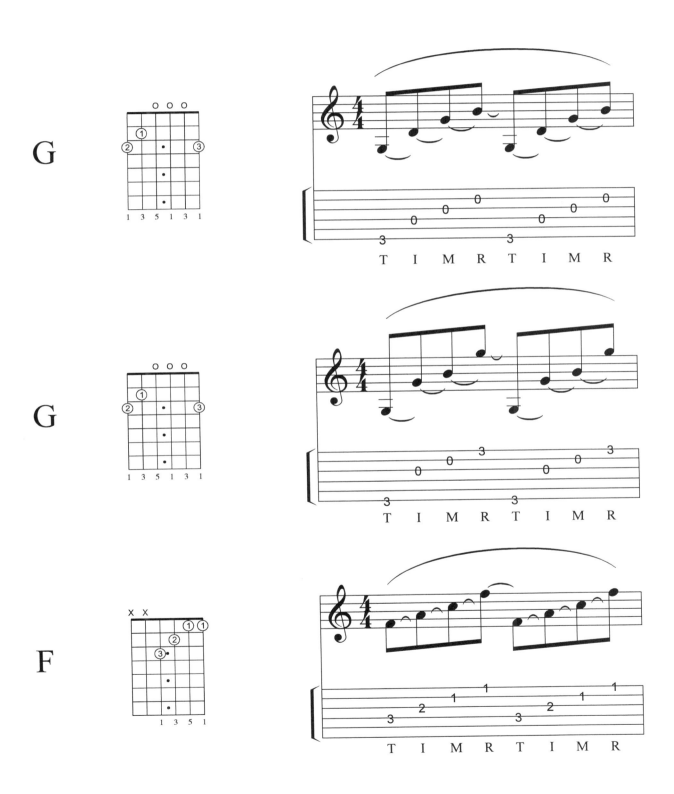

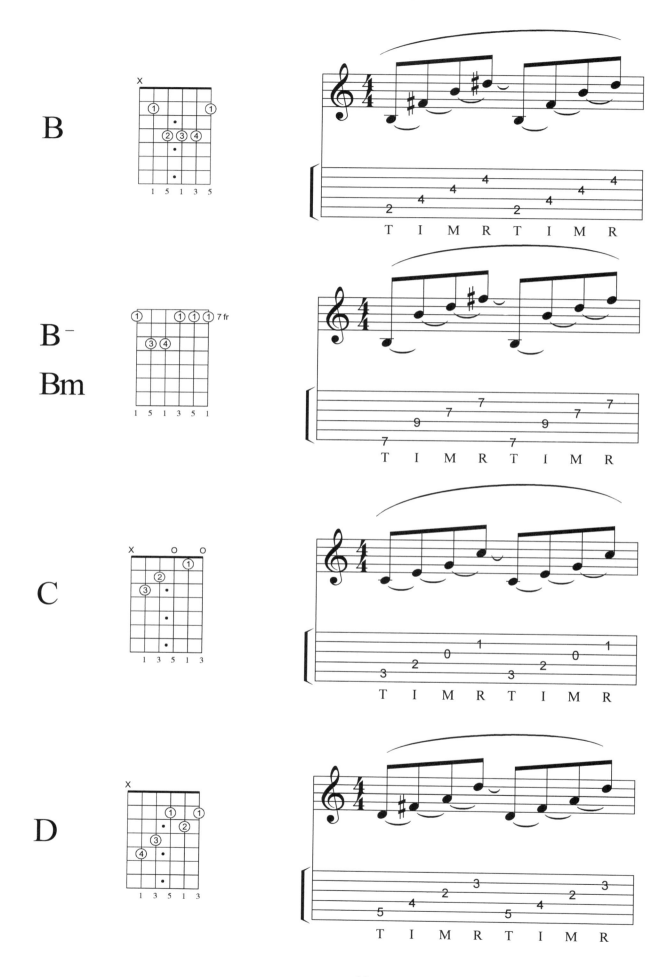

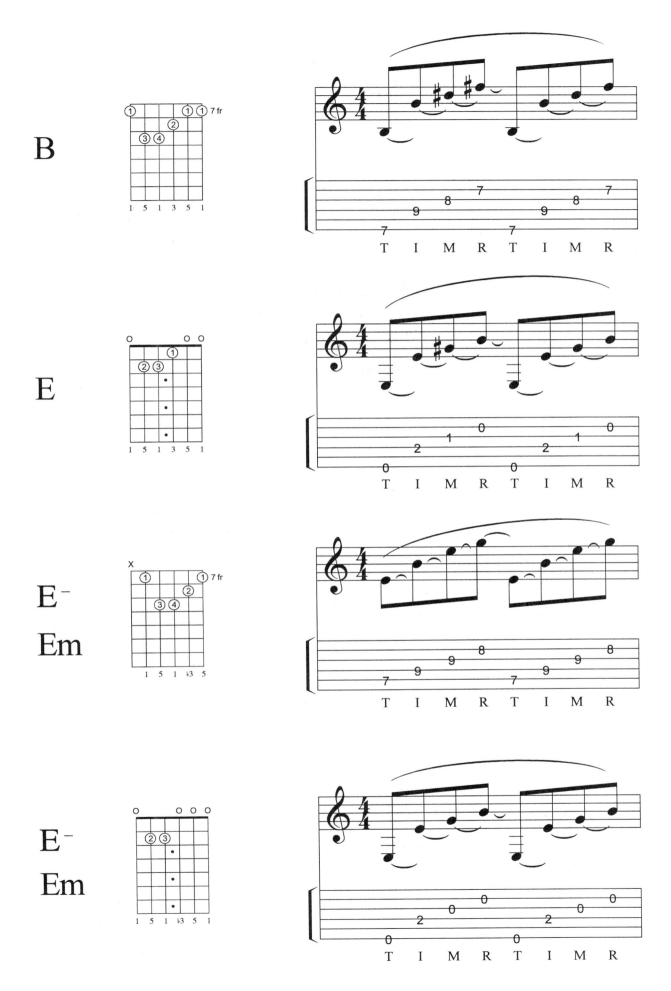

13

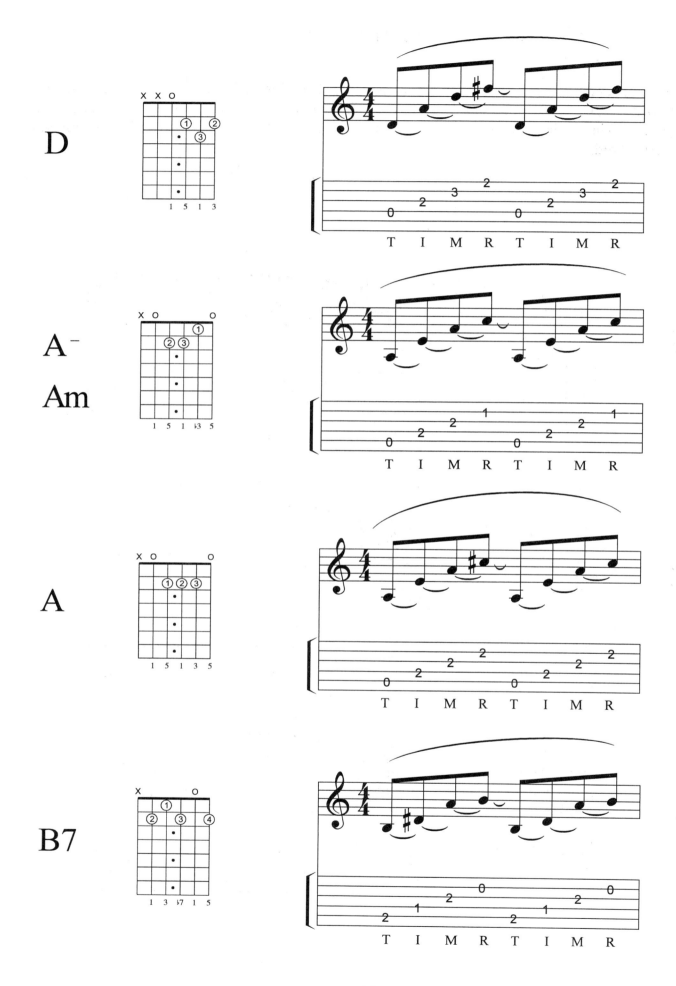

14

PATTERN 3

This next pattern is the first one we will study that is a little different than ascending and descending. Consider it a T, I, M, I, R, M, I, M pattern. This is also a four string pattern which means there are different ways of breaking up the pattern on chords using five or six strings. Again we have two different examples for the G chord.

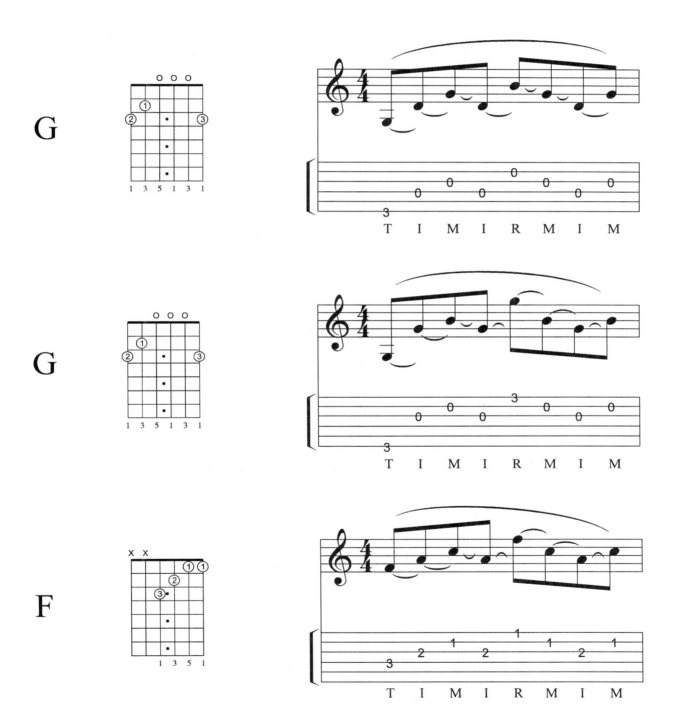

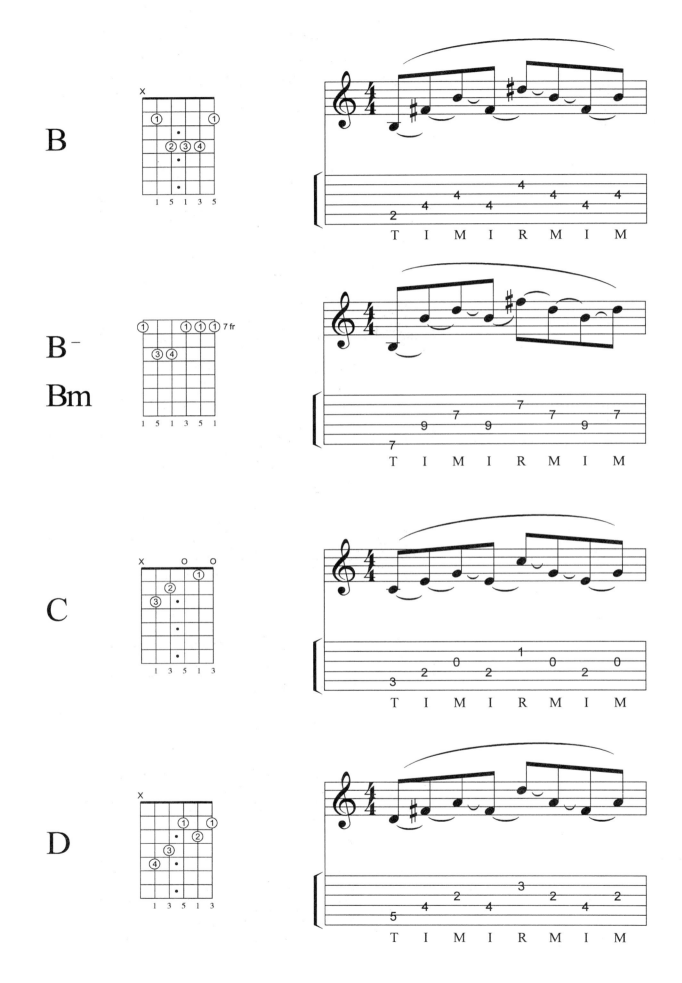

B

B[–]
Bm

C

D

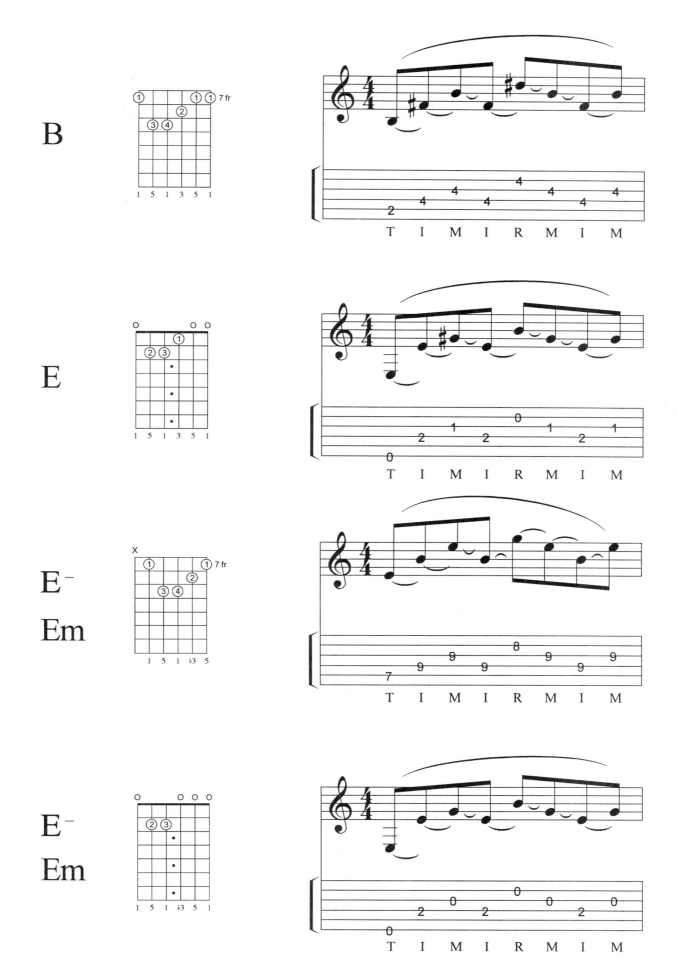

17

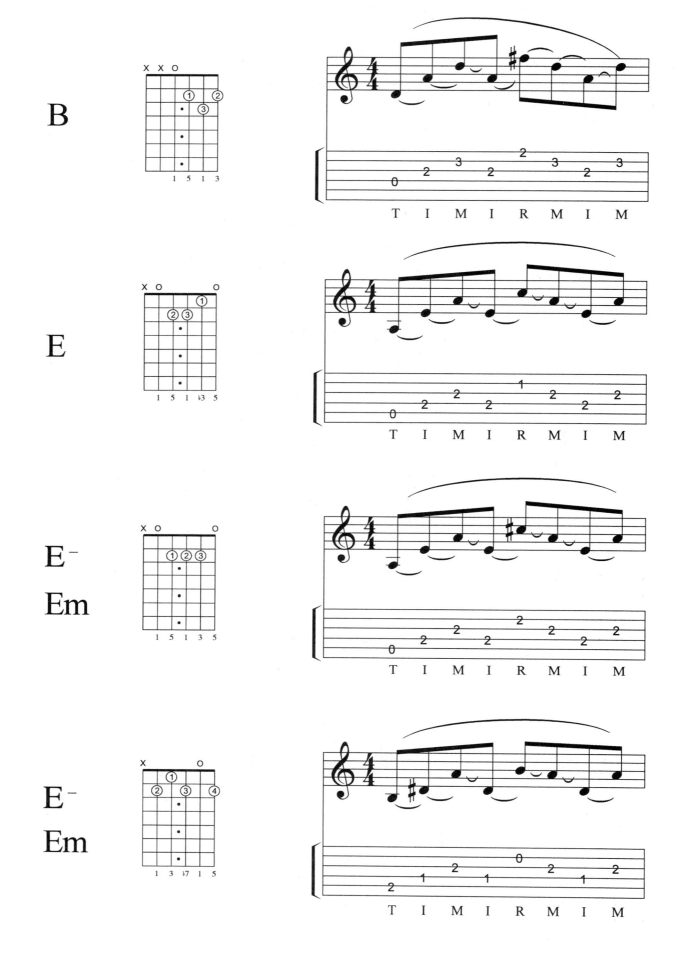

PATTERN 4

Pattern 4 is another ascending - descending pattern. This one is done in triplets. It is a T, I, M, R, M, I pattern. It is also a pattern that covers four strings which means there are different ways of fingerpicking chords that use five and six strings. Once again we give two ways of doing the G chord.

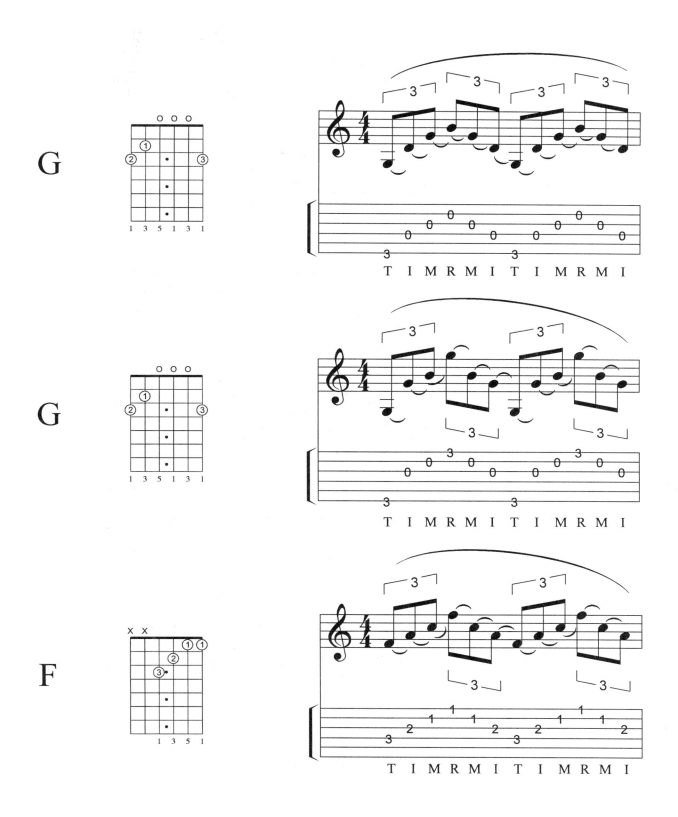

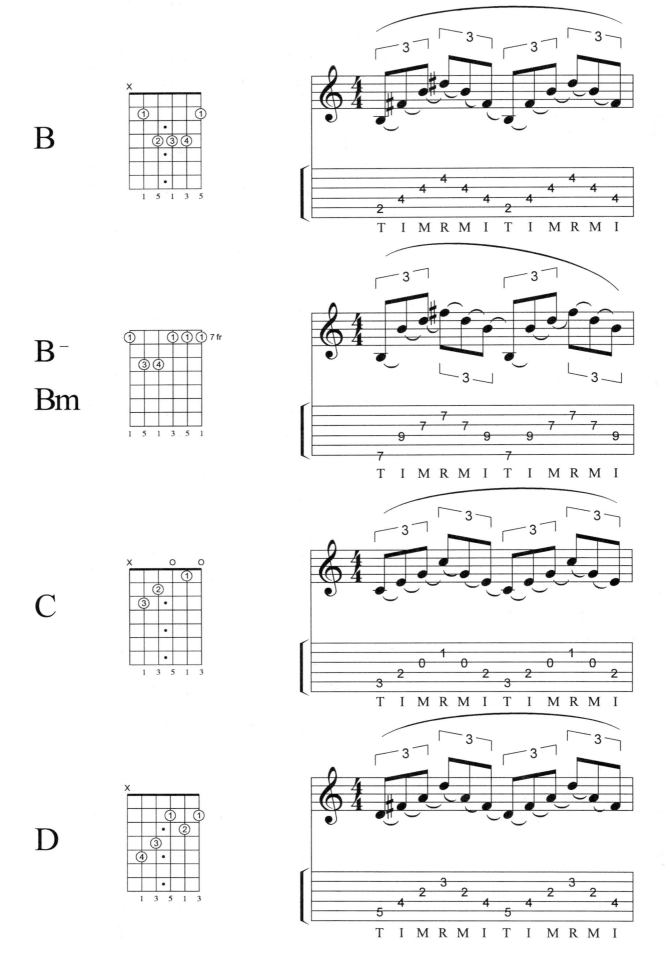

B

B⁻
Bm

C

D

20

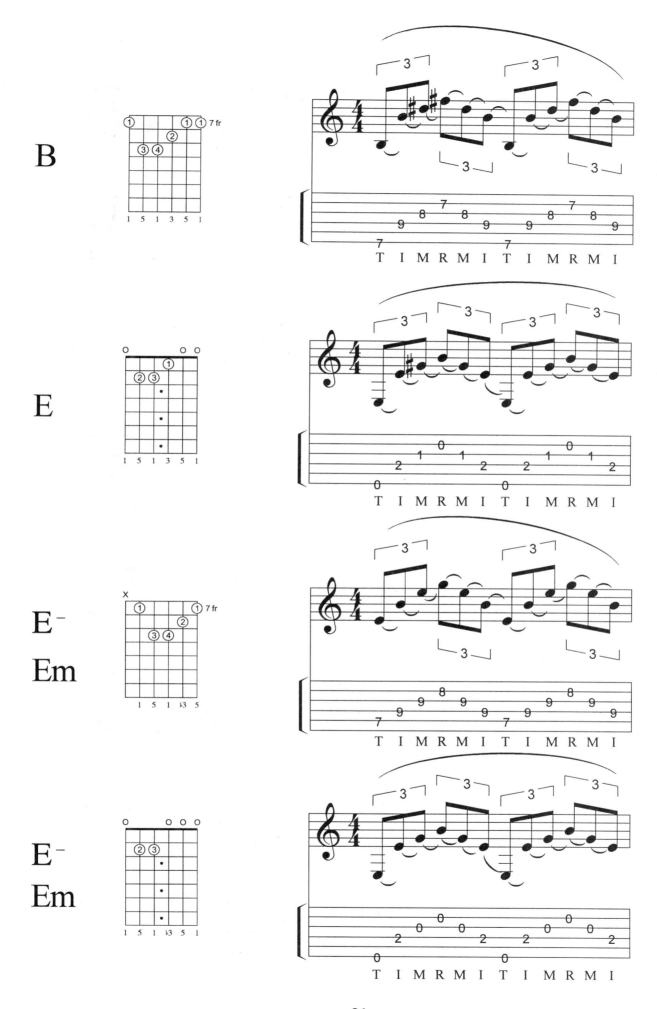

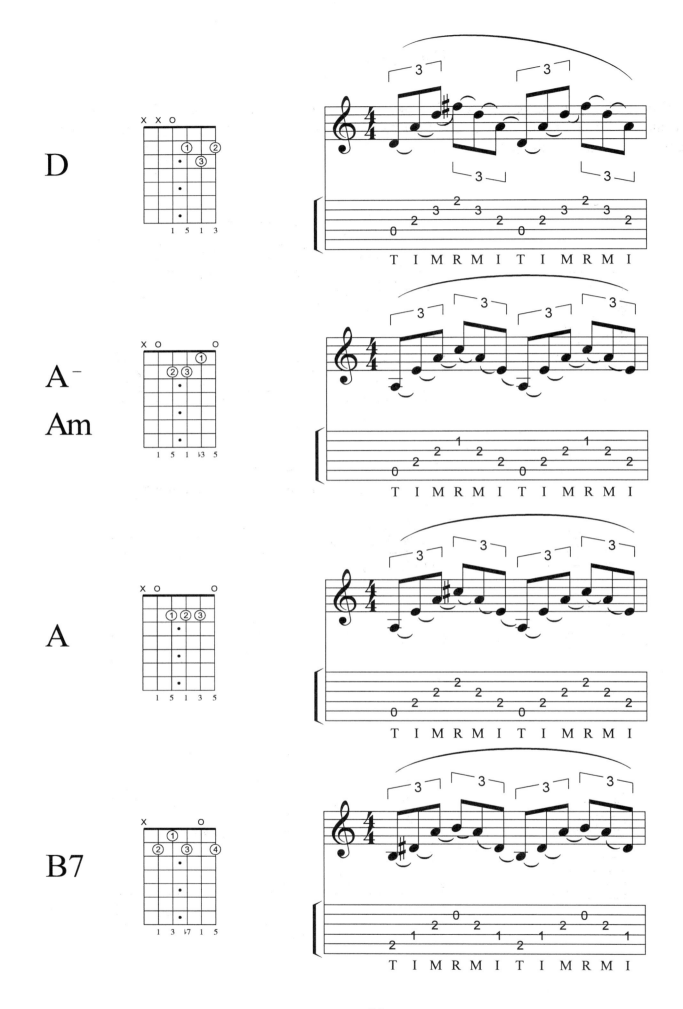

22

PATTERN 5

Pattern 5 is the first pattern we introduce that uses more than just single note strikes. The third note is actually an interval. This could be a T, I, (MR), I pattern. It is another four string pattern that is demonstrated two different ways using the G chord.

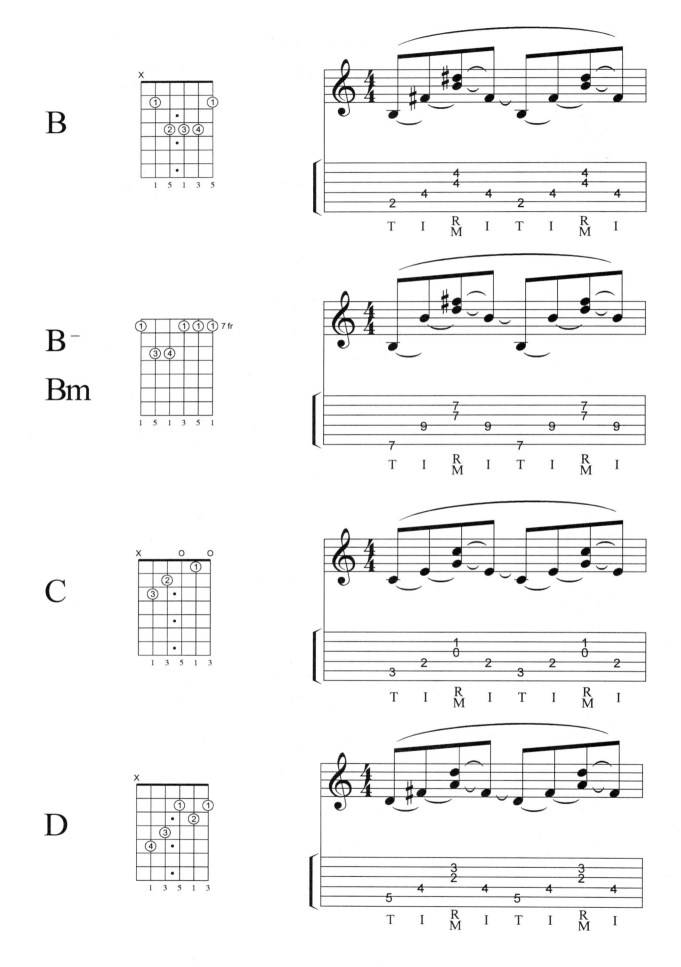

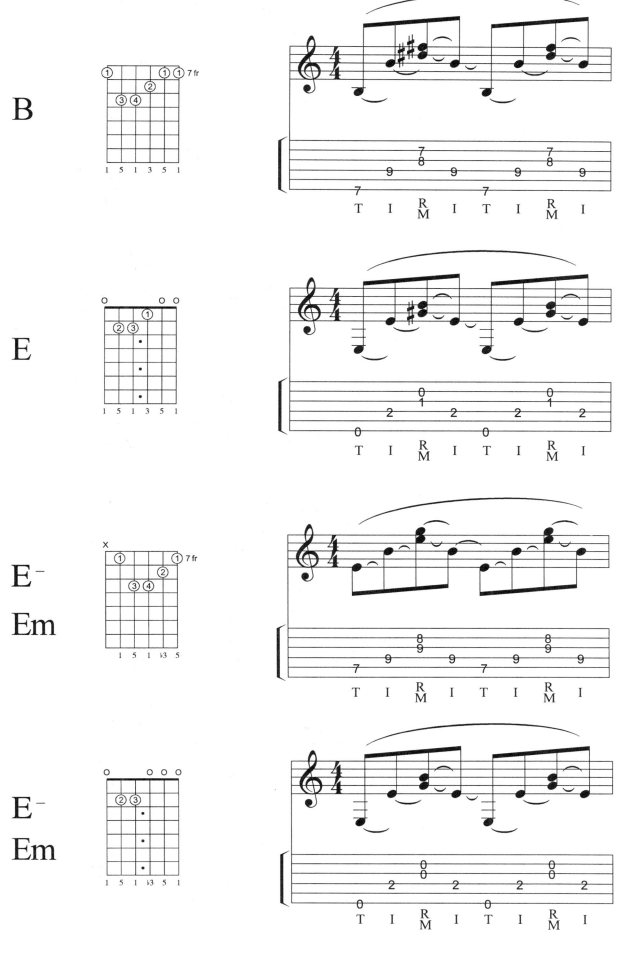

25

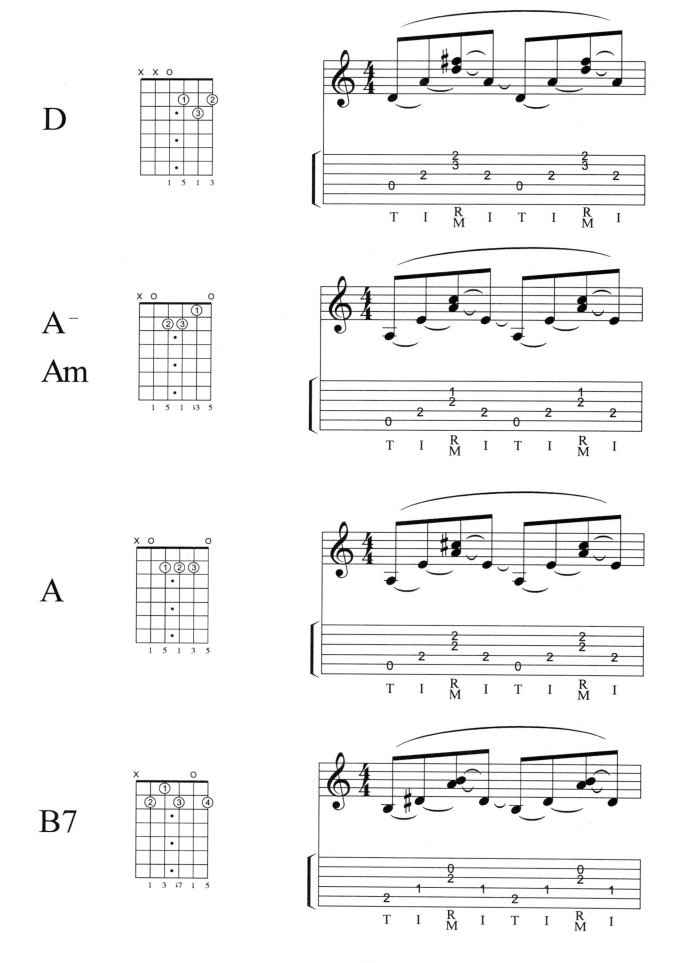

26

PATTERN 6

Pattern 6 not only uses an interval, but it is the first pattern mixing quarter and eigth notes. Also note that the interval is skipping strings. The interval is played with the thumb which means the thumb is being used twice in a row. We can look at this pattern as a T, (T,M) T, M, I, R pattern. In the second example using the G chord we skip two strings to show you that there are quite a few ways to play the same pattern.

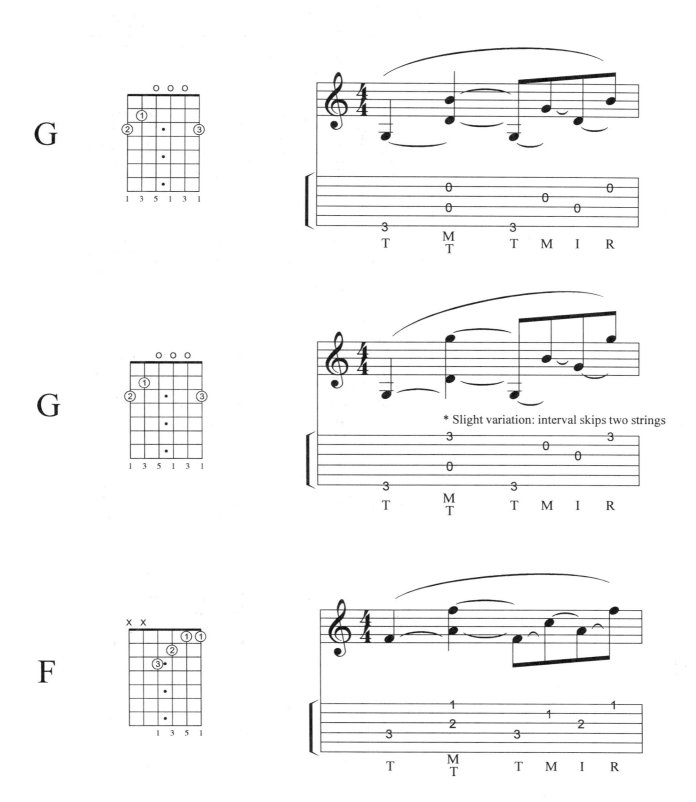

* Slight variation: interval skips two strings

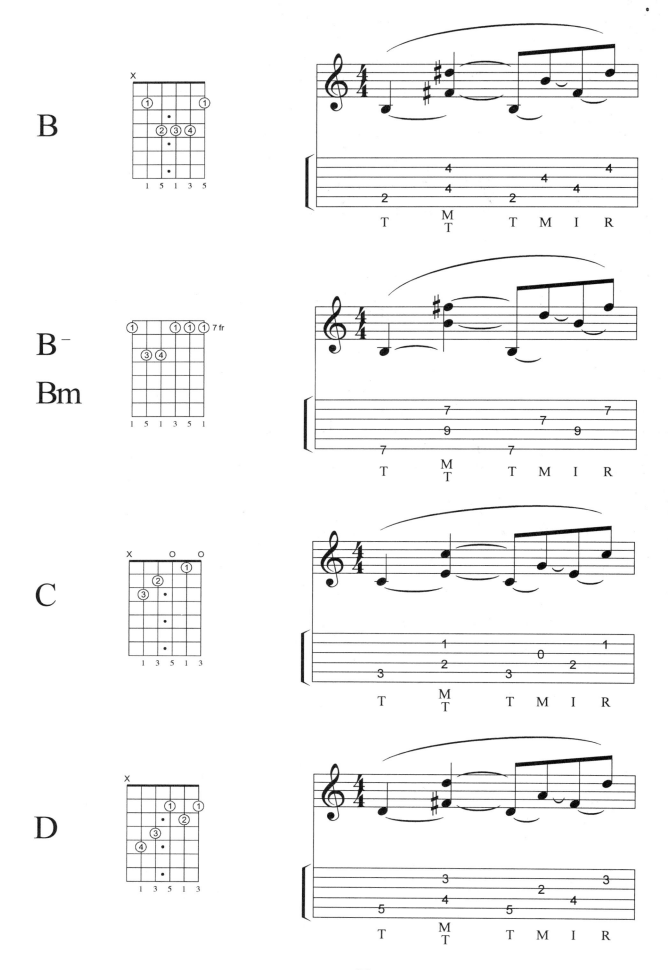

B

B⁻
Bm

C

D

28

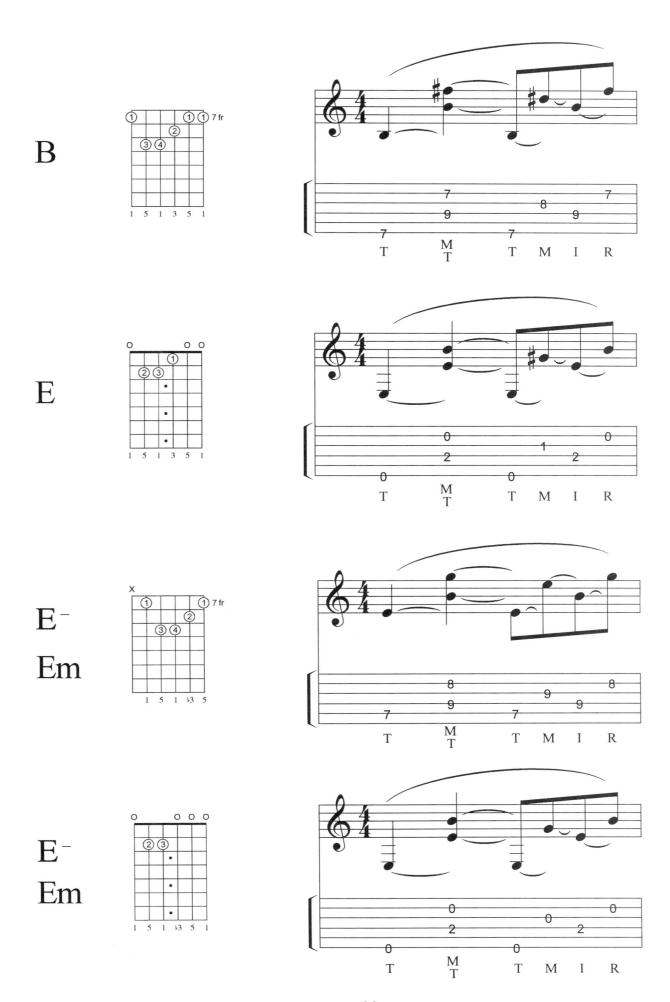

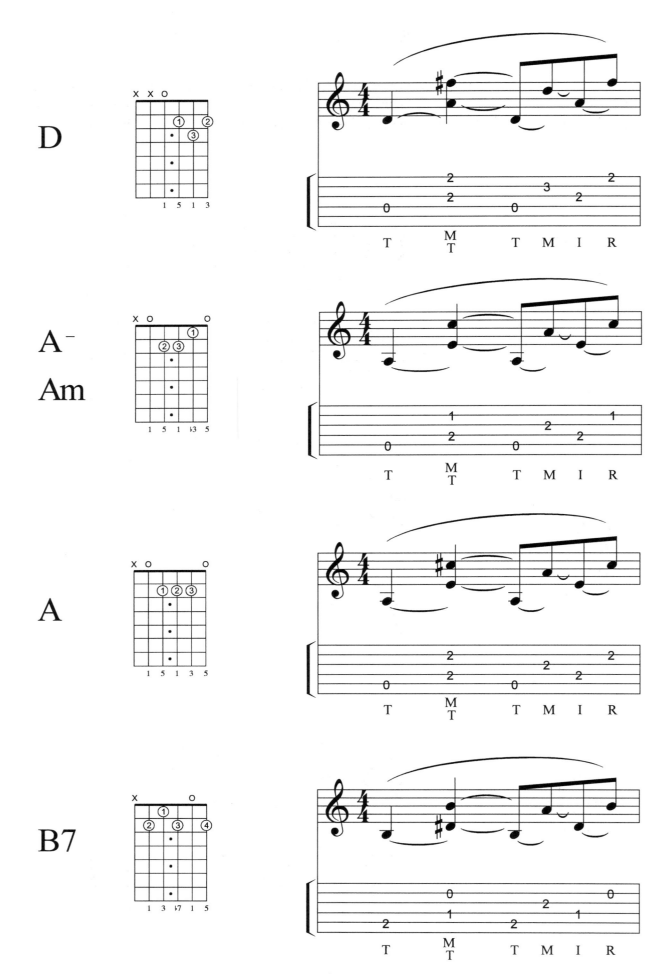

PATTERN 7

Pattern 7 is another straight ascending-descending pattern. It is done in $\frac{3}{4}$ time. It is a T, I, M, R, M, I pattern. It covers four strings which means again that there are different ways of playing chords that use five or six strings. And once again the G chord is used to give you two examples of playing this pattern.

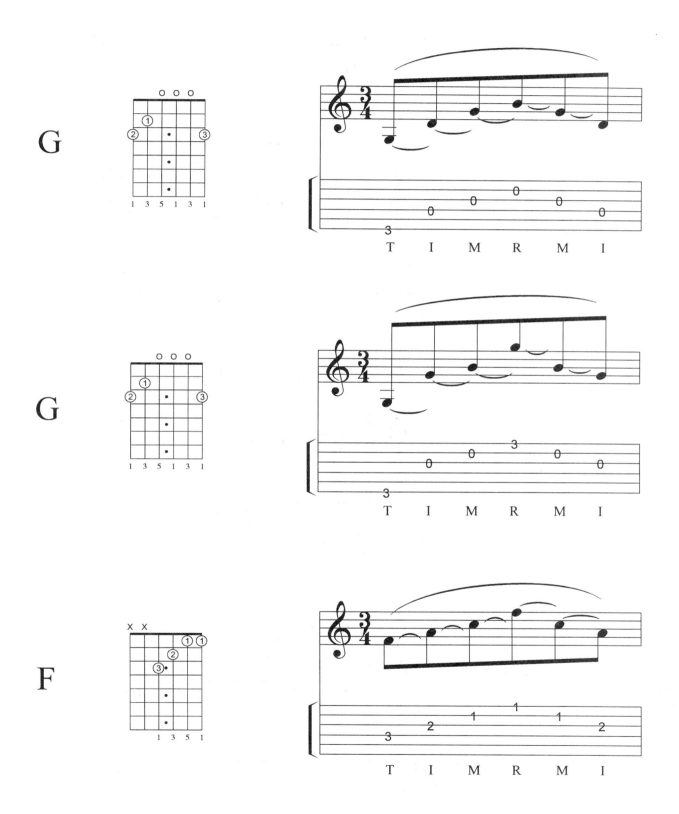

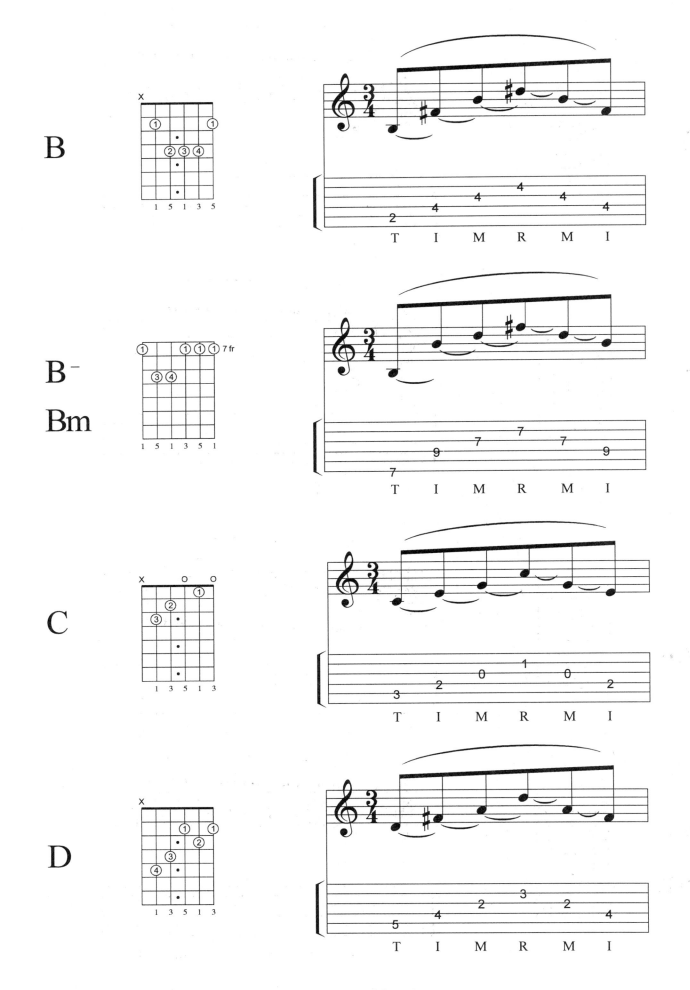

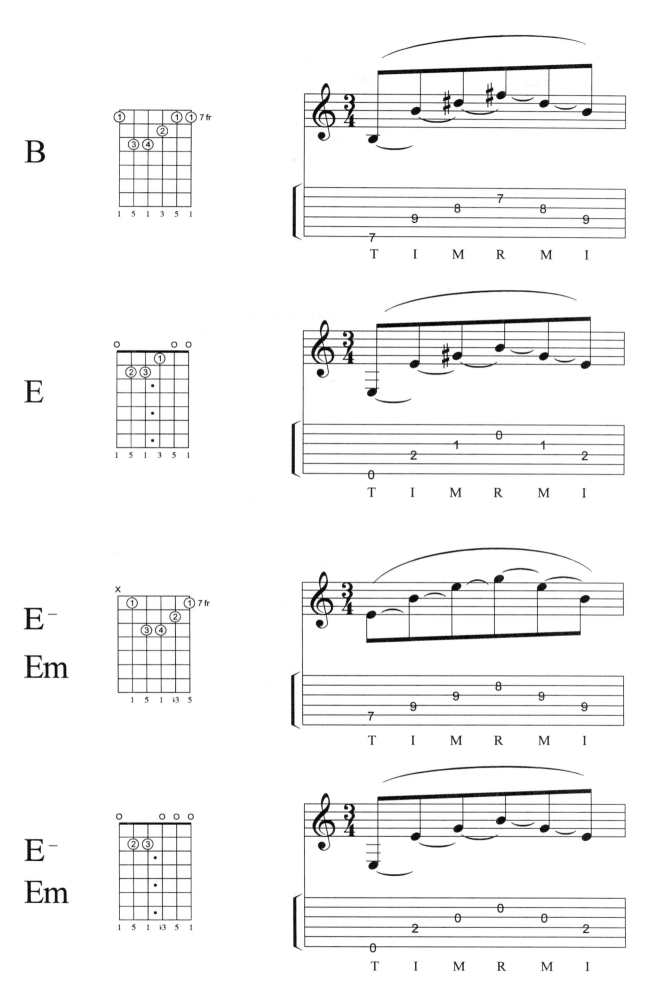

33

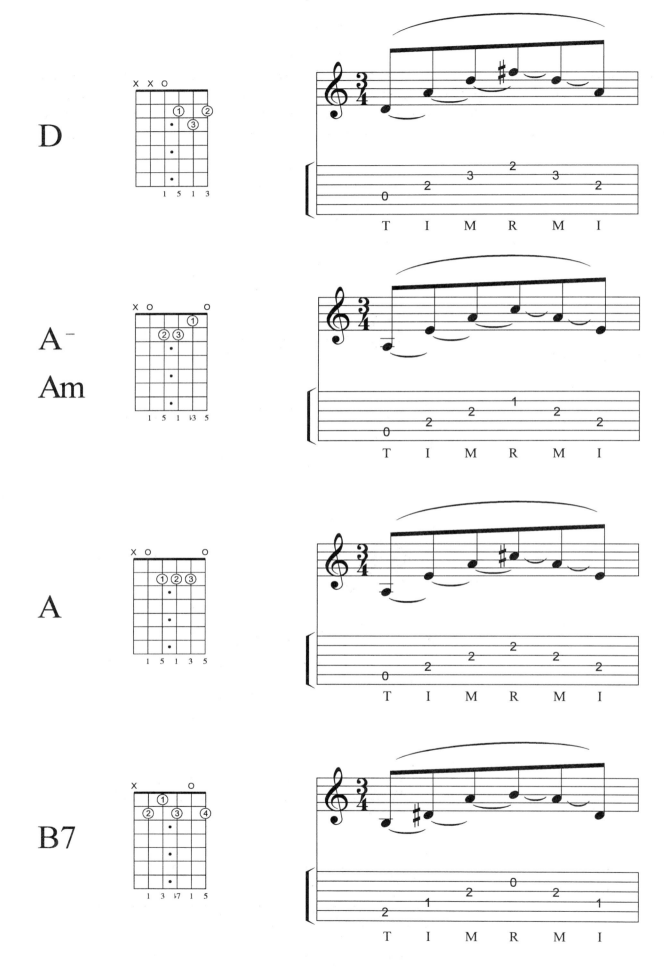

34

PATTERN 8

Pattern 8 is a chord with a one, five (root fifth) bass pattern, if you will. It is a T(I M R) pattern. It covers four strings which means again that there are different ways of playing chords that use five or six strings. And once again the G chord is used to give you two examples of playing this pattern. You hit the root note bass first, then the chord, then the fifth. The fifth will sometimes be below the root and sometimes above the root.

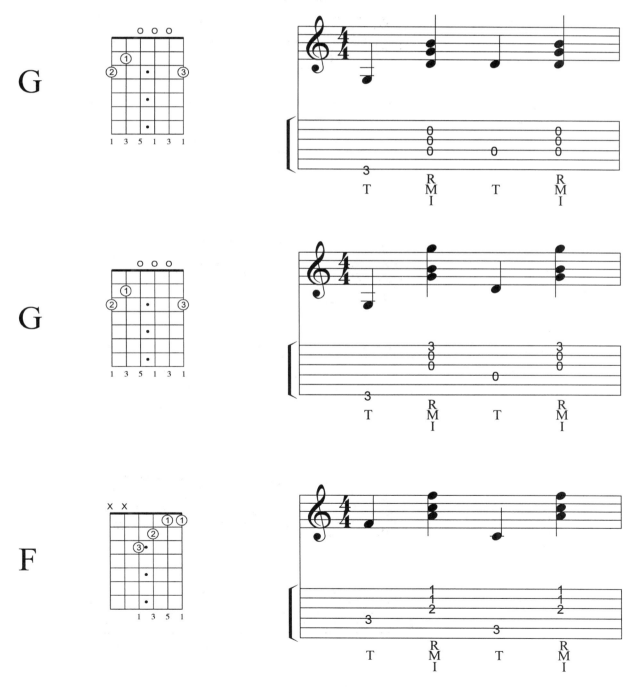

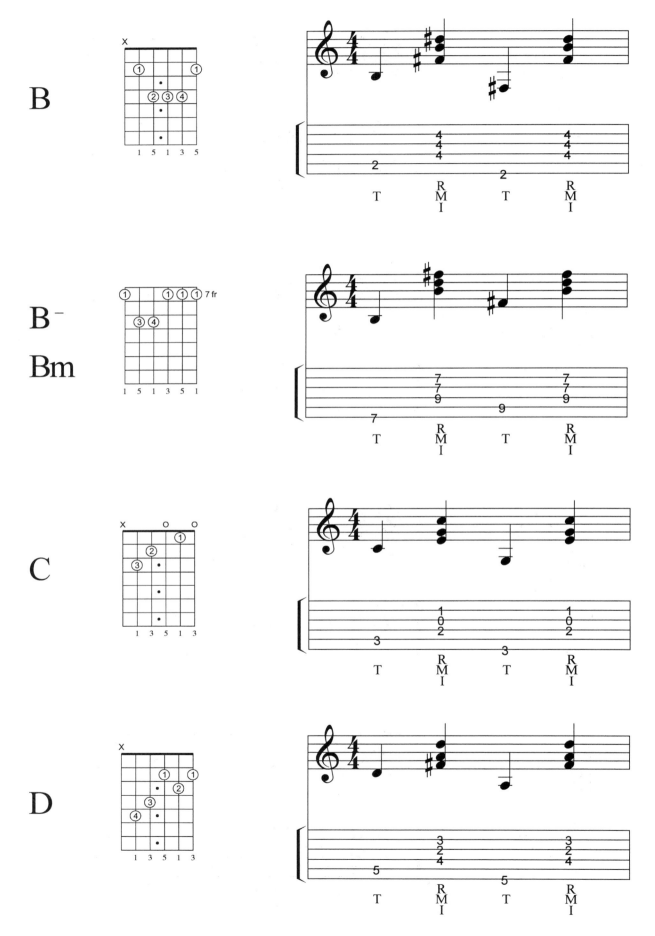

B

B⁻
Bm

C

D

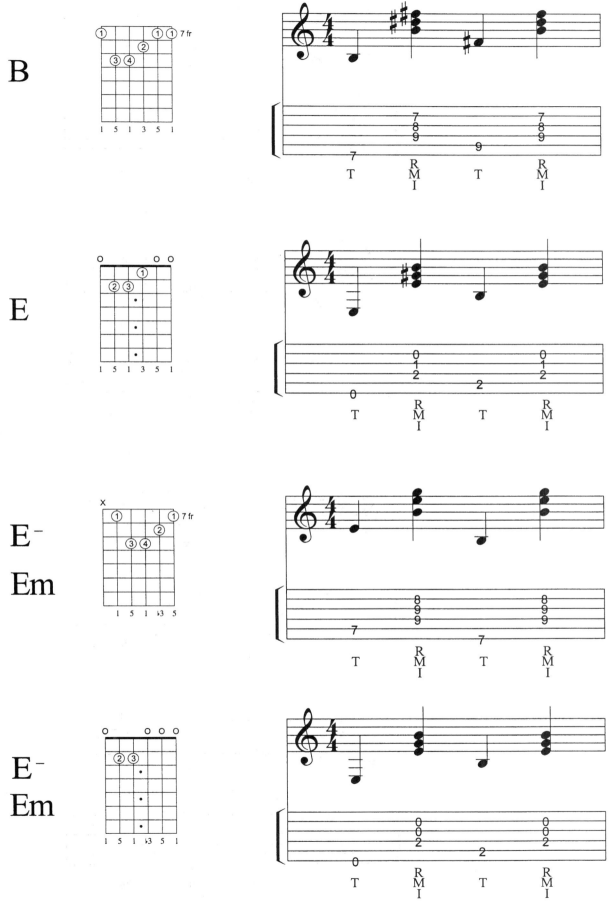

B

E

E⁻
Em

E⁻
Em

37

D

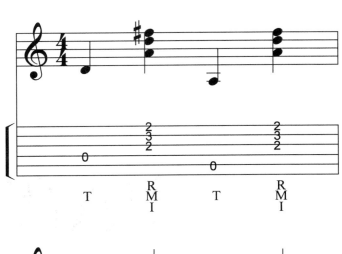

A⁻
Am

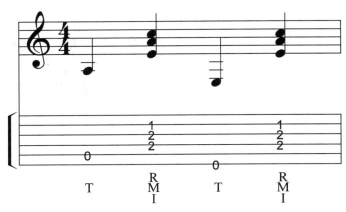

A

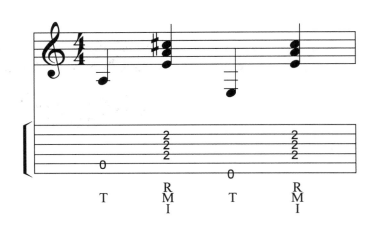

B7

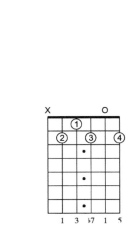
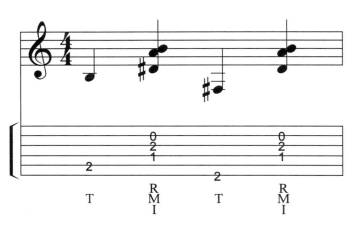

PART TWO

SCALE FINGERPICKING
(Major)

FINGERPICKING THE SCALES

We are going to start with the F Major scale. The reason we are starting with F is because the patterns connect nicely starting with pattern 1. What I mean is, other keys may start with pattern 5 for instance, and connect thus: 5, 6, 7, 1, 2, 3, 4. But we will get to that later, for now just concern yourself with F Major.

Below we have figure 4 demonstrating the key of F Major as it applies to the fretboard. The fretboard to the far left shows every note possible, and the fretboards to the right of that show how to break it down into patterns making it easier for us to play since we don't have 30 fingers on our hands.

Below that the individual patterns are expanded to demonstrate the fingering used to play each pattern.

F MAJOR

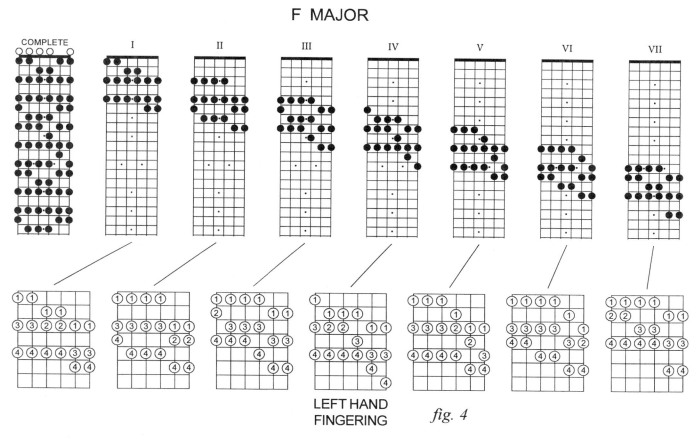

LEFT HAND
FINGERING   *fig. 4*

Though the notes may change when you move the position of the pattern to change keys, the fingering and the intervallic relationship remain the same (fig. 5). If you don't understand intervals we recommend **The Guitar Grimoire Scales & Modes.**

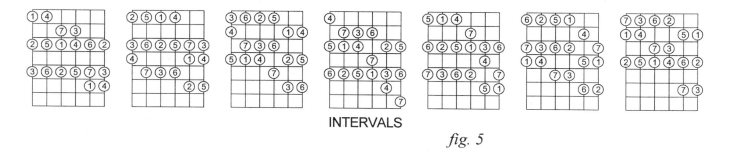

INTERVALS

fig. 5

The notes in F Major for the patterns are as follows.

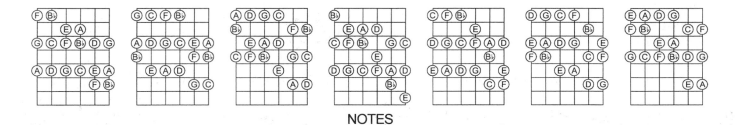

NOTES

The symbols are the same as for fingerpicking the chords, T for thumb, I for index finger, M for middle finger, R for ring finger and P for pinky. These are the ascending picking patterns, in other words, from the lowest note to the highest note consecutively.

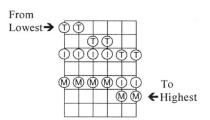

Note that all seven patterns are the same as far as T, I, M etc. even though they are fingered differently. In fact, once mastered, you use the same patterns for any of the seven tone exotic scales from the **Guitar Grimoire Scales & Modes.**

I	II	III	IV	V	VI	VII

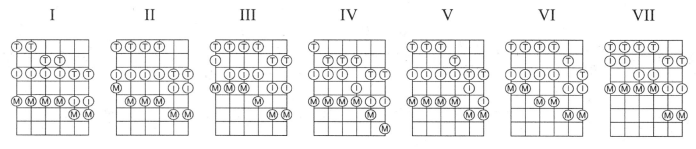

ASCENDING PICKING PATTERN

PATTERNS IN F MAJOR (ascending)

I

I notated this exercise in 18/8 time so you can see the strings in 3 note groups and so the entire pattern would fit in one measure.

Observe the picking pattern above the notes.

II

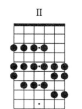

Pick the notes evenly and smoothly. Remember that the picking pattern is the same for each fingering pattern in each measure.

T I M T I M T I M T I M T I M T I M   T I M T I M T I M T I M T I M T I M

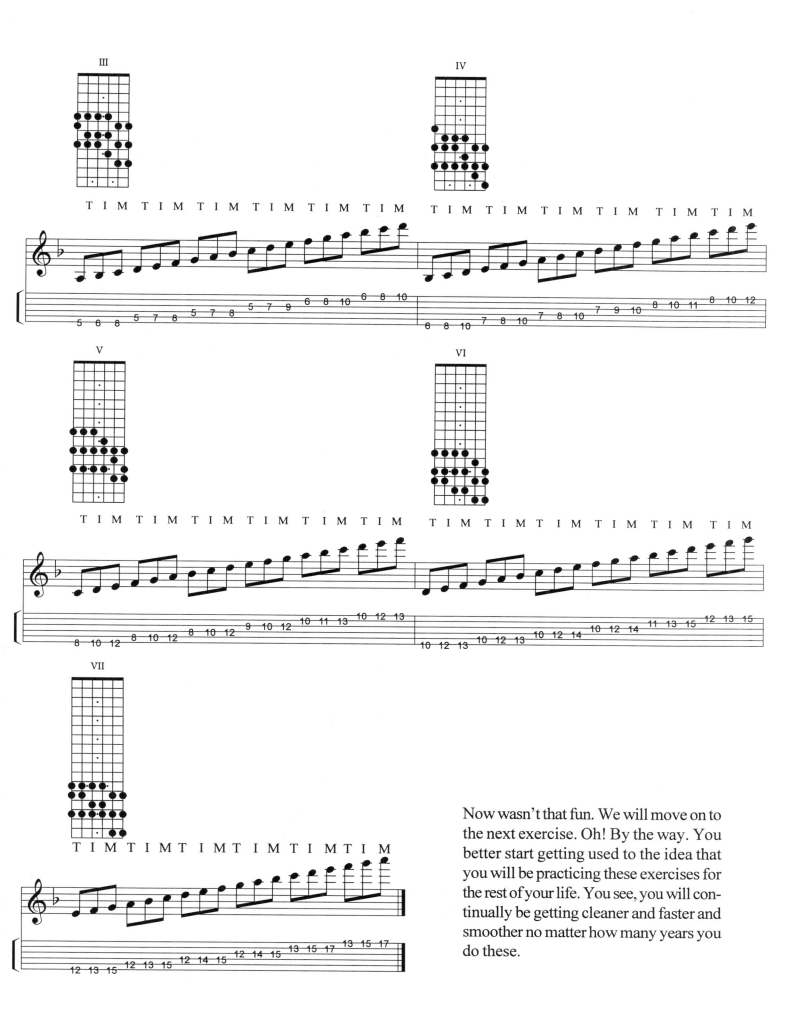

Now wasn't that fun. We will move on to the next exercise. Oh! By the way. You better start getting used to the idea that you will be practicing these exercises for the rest of your life. You see, you will continually be getting cleaner and faster and smoother no matter how many years you do these.

43

Next we go to the descending fingerpicking patterns. In this case we go from the highest note to the lowest.

Just as with the ascending, the fingerpicking pattern for all seven fingering patterns is the same. In fact the right hand fingering is the same as the ascending.

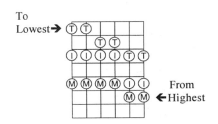

I II III IV V VI VII

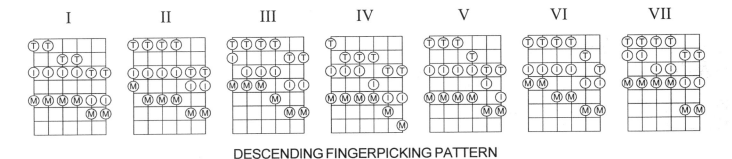

DESCENDING FINGERPICKING PATTERN

PATTERNS IN F MAJOR (descending)

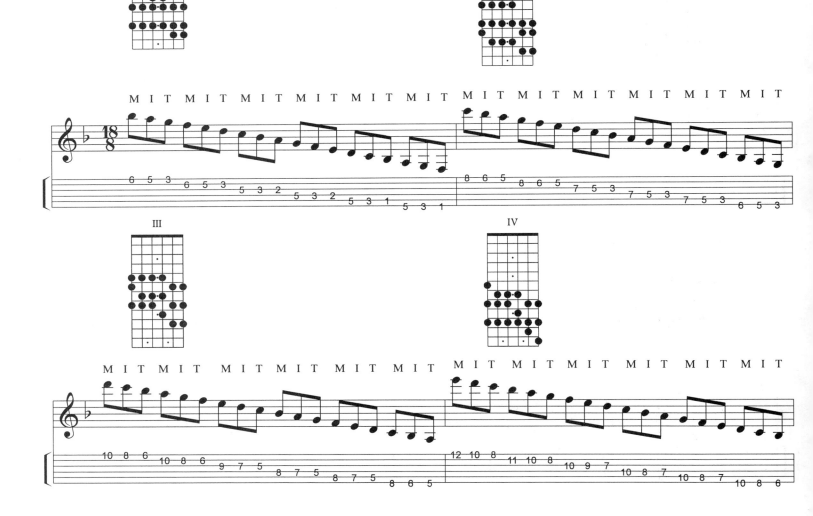

44

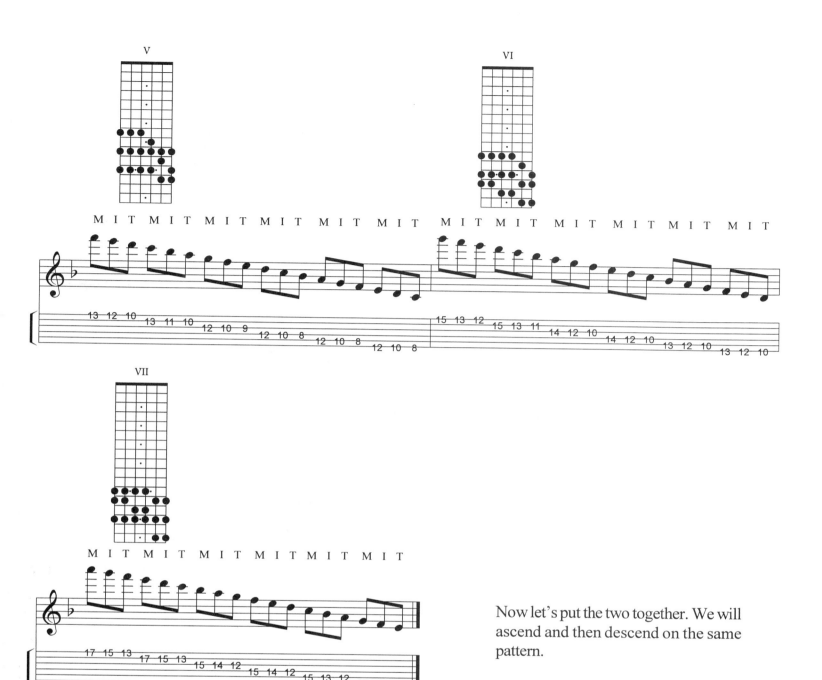

Now let's put the two together. We will ascend and then descend on the same pattern.

PATTERNS IN F MAJOR (ascending & descending)

We use the ascending fingerpicking here.   We use the descending fingerpicking here.

45

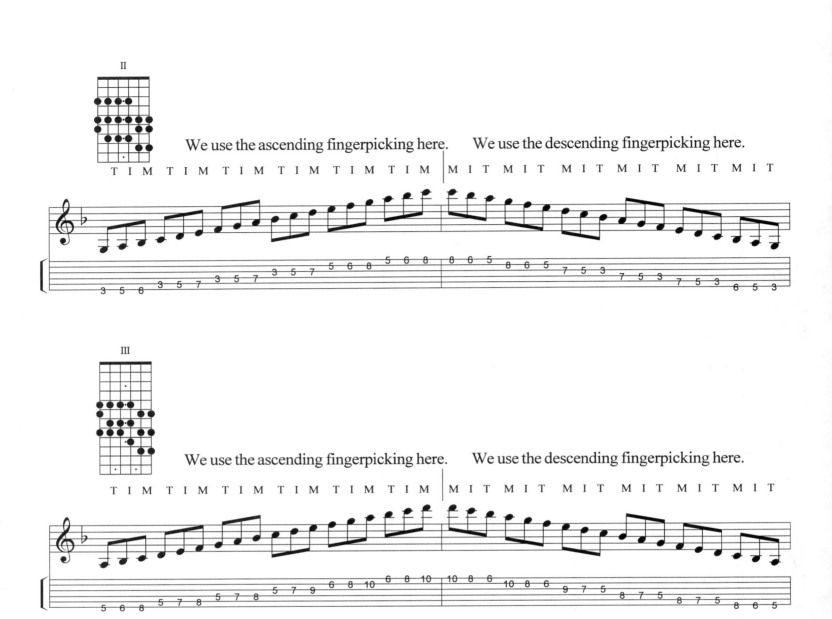

We use the ascending fingerpicking here.   We use the descending fingerpicking here.

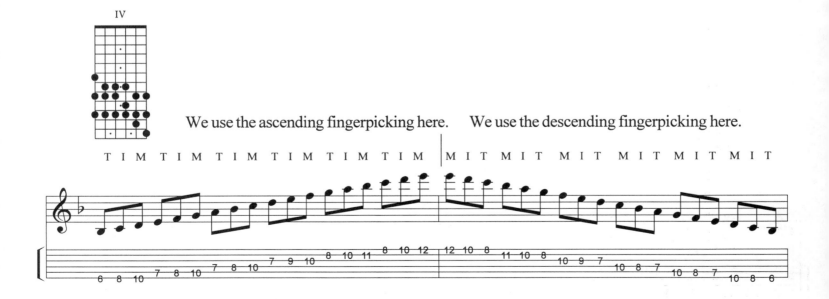

We use the ascending fingerpicking here.   We use the descending fingerpicking here.

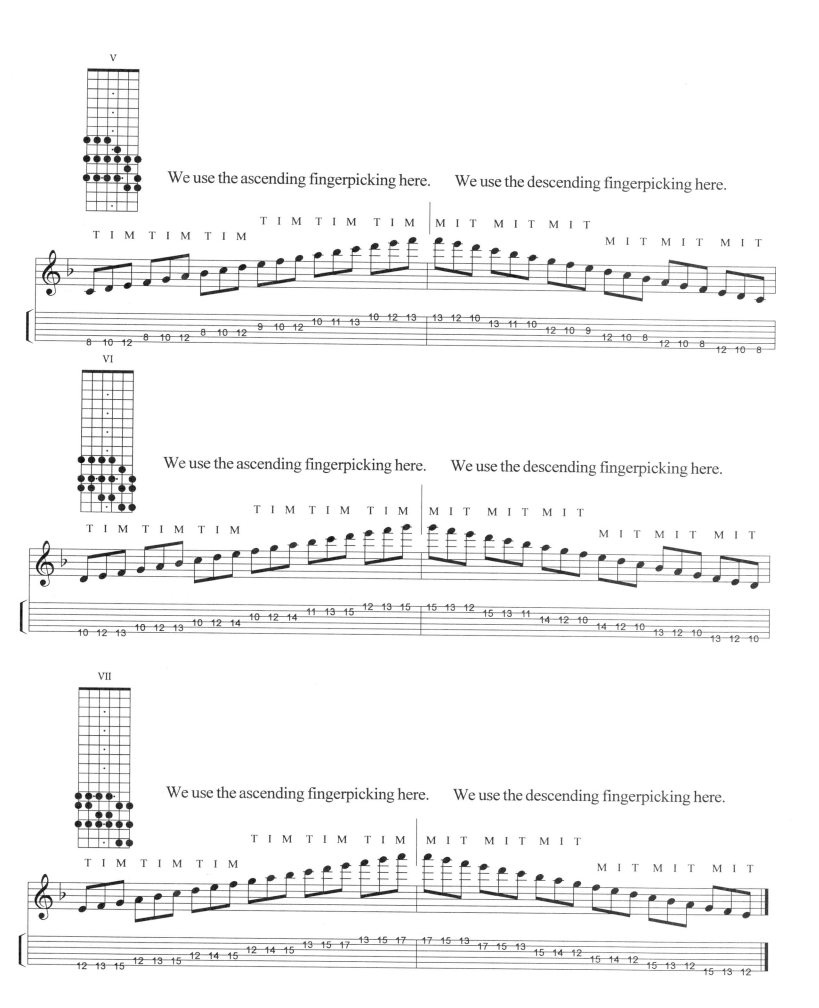

PATTERNS IN F MAJOR (ascending & descending - alternating)

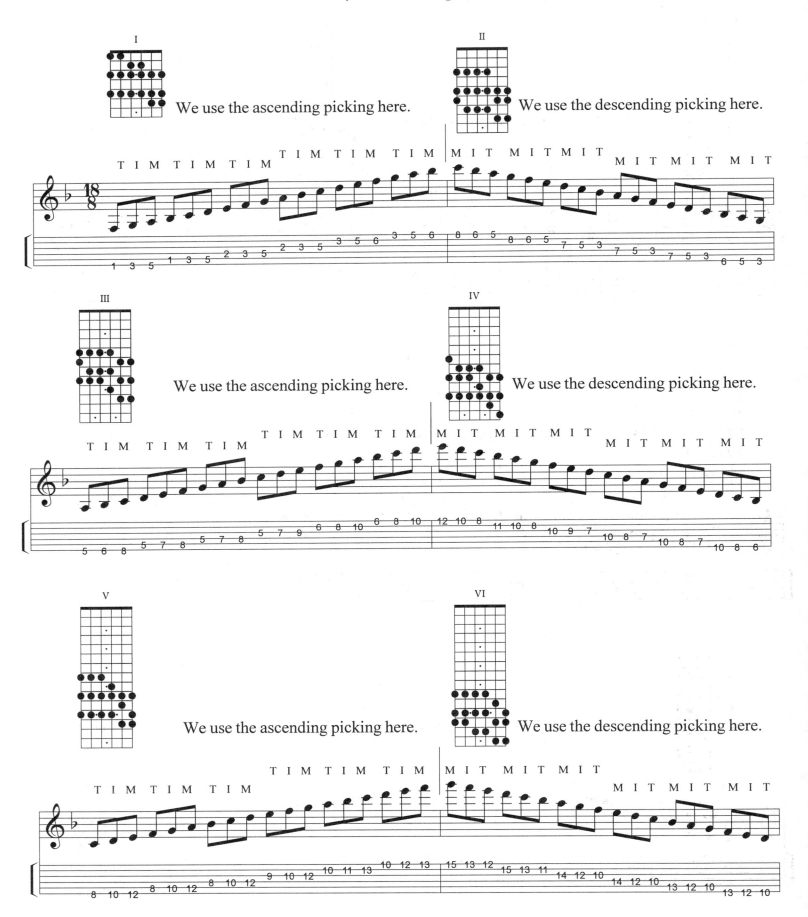

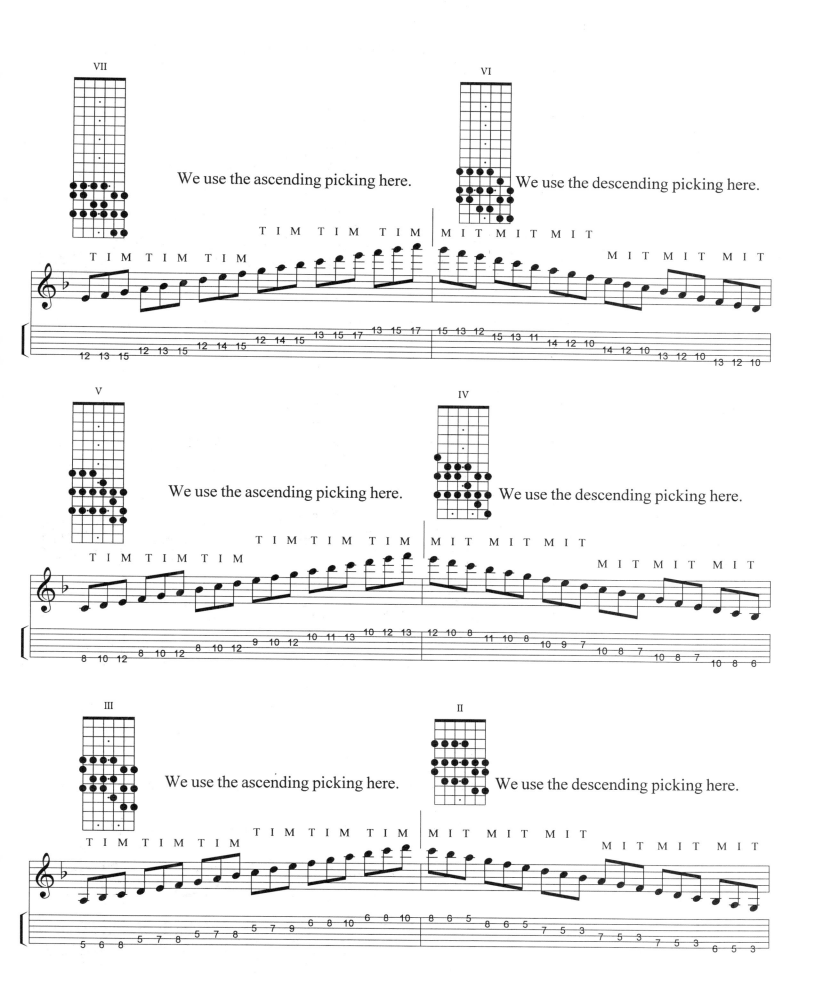

49

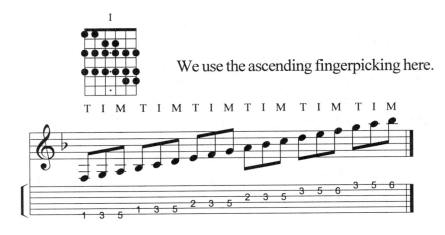

We use the ascending fingerpicking here.

COILS

Now we are going to cover coils. First of all let's discuss what a coil is for those of you who have never heard of them. Some texts have called them spirals and others by other names. In a nutshell coils ascend or descend in groups of three or four or even five or six. The following group starts on the second tone of the group preceding it. It will make more sense once we start.

First we have to learn the fingerpicking patterns. In order to learn the fingerpicking pattern for each fingering pattern we have to break it up into "mini" patterns. The notes darkened in the fretboard pattern above each measure are the notes used from the fingering pattern for that measure.

Once learned and mastered, coils add style when thrown into your solos. We are going to start with three note coils.

THREE NOTE COIL ASCENDING PICKING PATTERNS

We are going to start by breaking down pattern 1 of the Major scale in three note coil format. Below, each group of three represents a "mini" pattern of two strings. Each group also represents measures in the exercise with an oddball pattern for the last measure of each line. I notated these in 9/8 time with an oddball of 3/8 time so each measure could clearly demonstrate each "mini" picking pattern. Notice the fingerpicking pattern of T,I,M, T,I,M, T,I,M repeats with each measure and the oddball pattern is also T,I,M. Remember that the fingerpicking is identical for all the patterns of the Major scale.

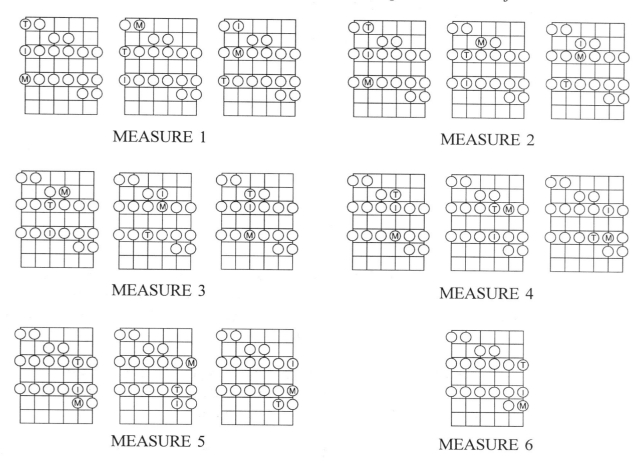

MEASURE 1   MEASURE 2

MEASURE 3   MEASURE 4

MEASURE 5   MEASURE 6

THREE NOTE COILS IN F MAJOR (ascending)

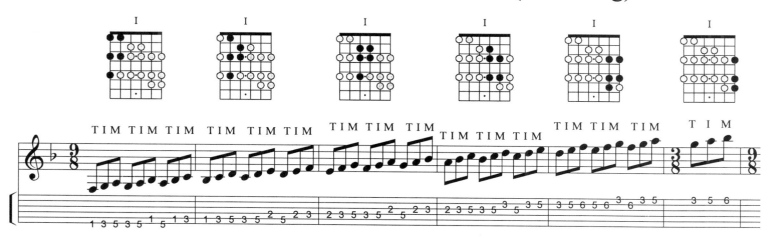

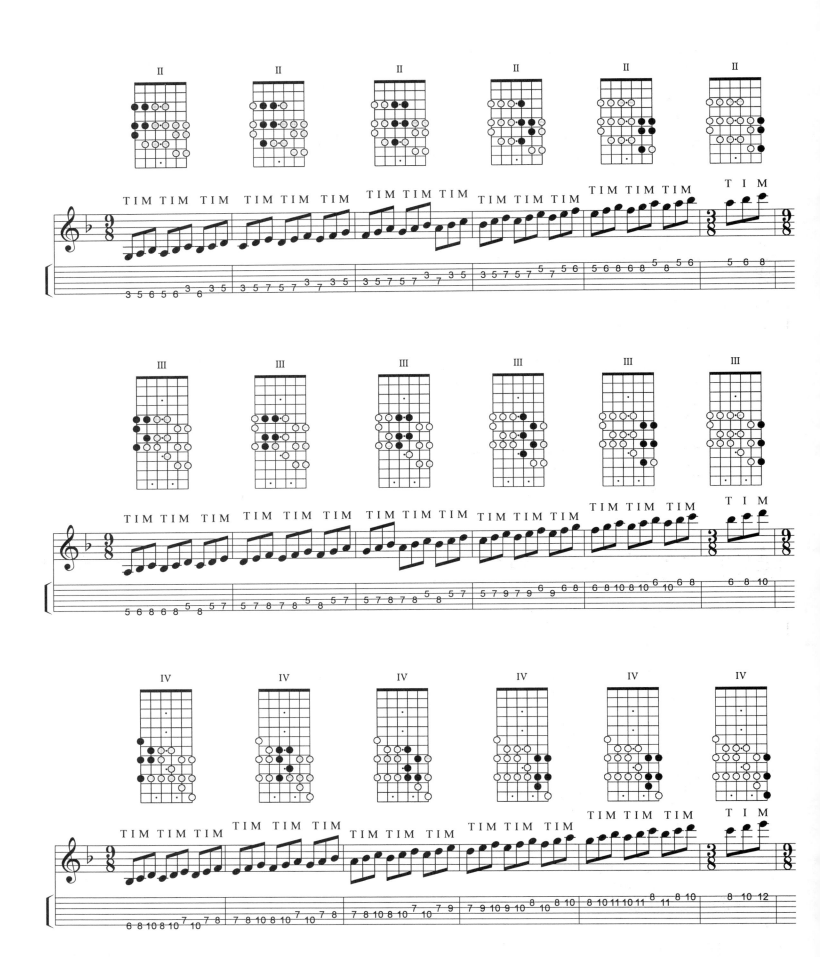

52

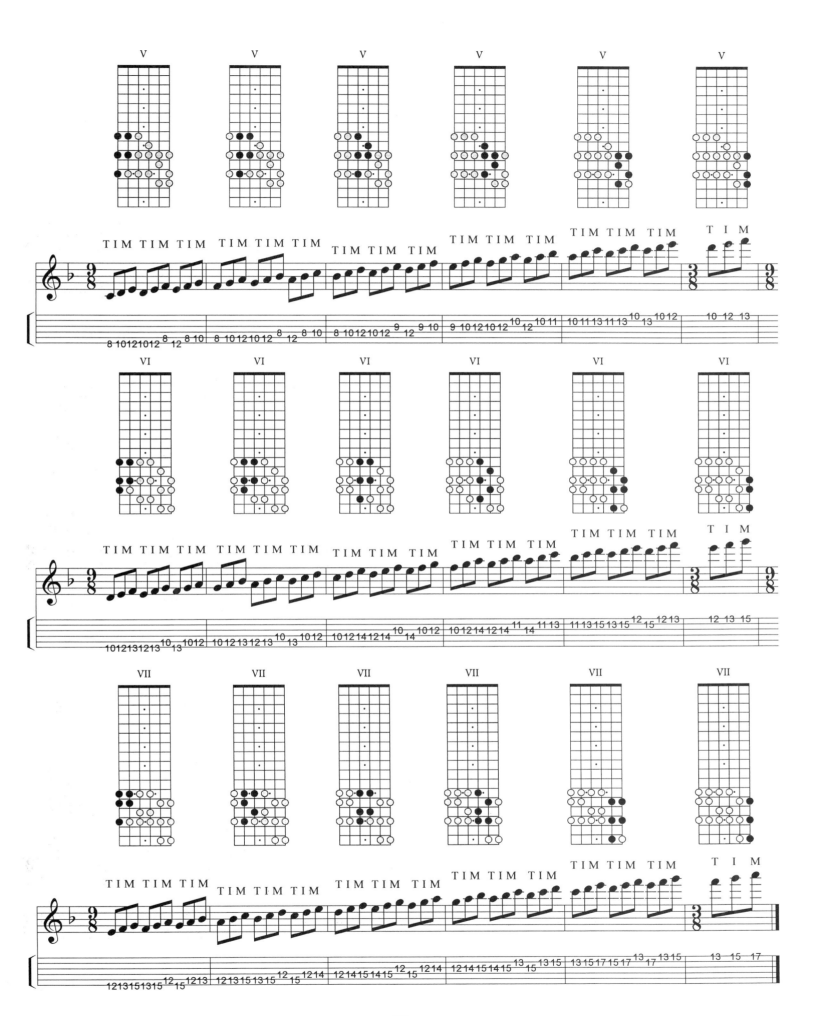

THREE NOTE COIL DESCENDING PICKING PATTERNS

The fingerpicking pattern for the three note coils descending is the same as ascending just in reverse.

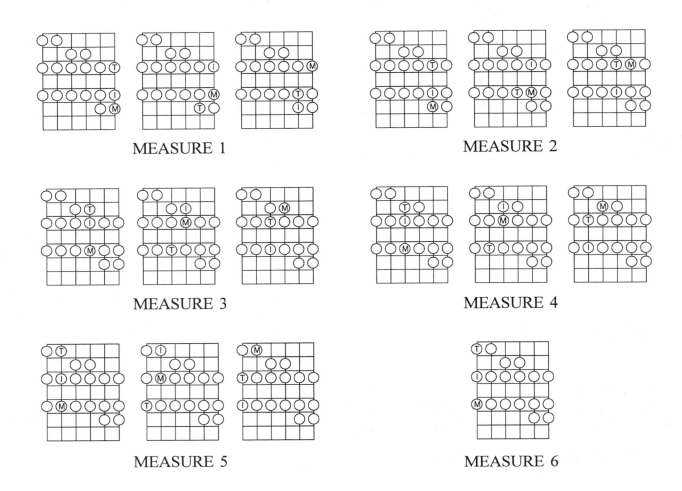

MEASURE 1   MEASURE 2

MEASURE 3   MEASURE 4

MEASURE 5   MEASURE 6

THREE NOTE COILS IN F MAJOR (descending)

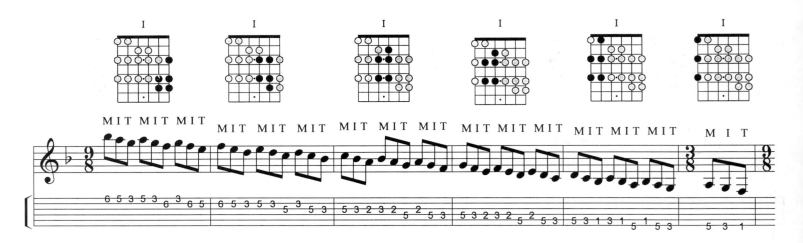

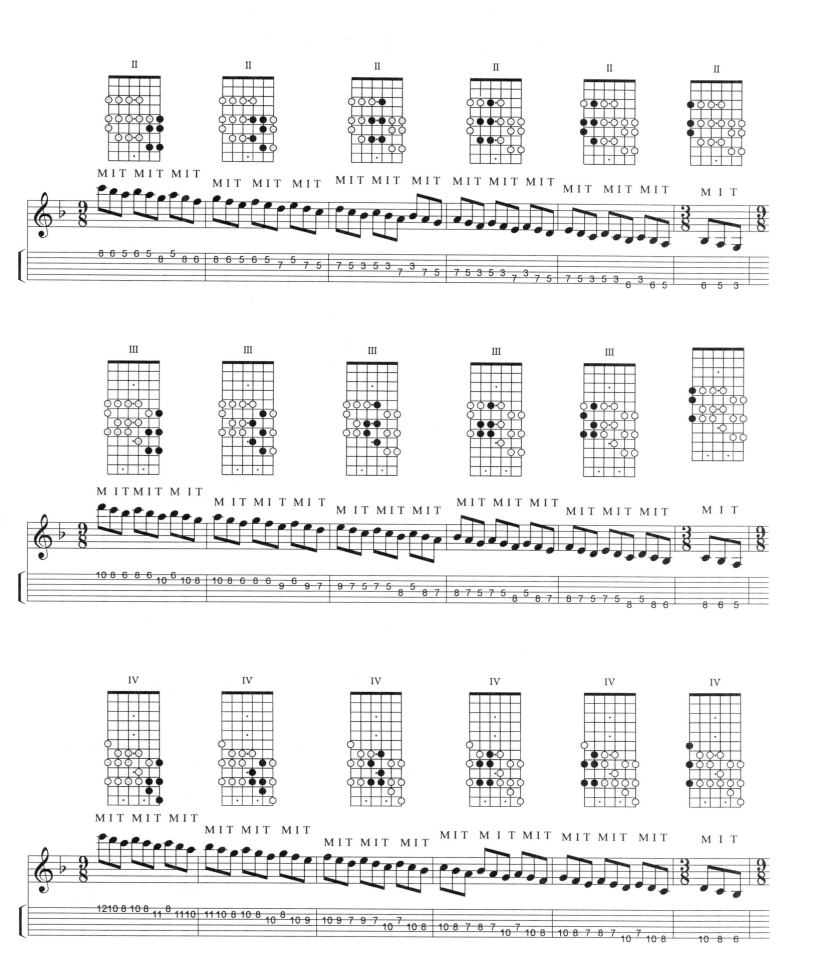

55

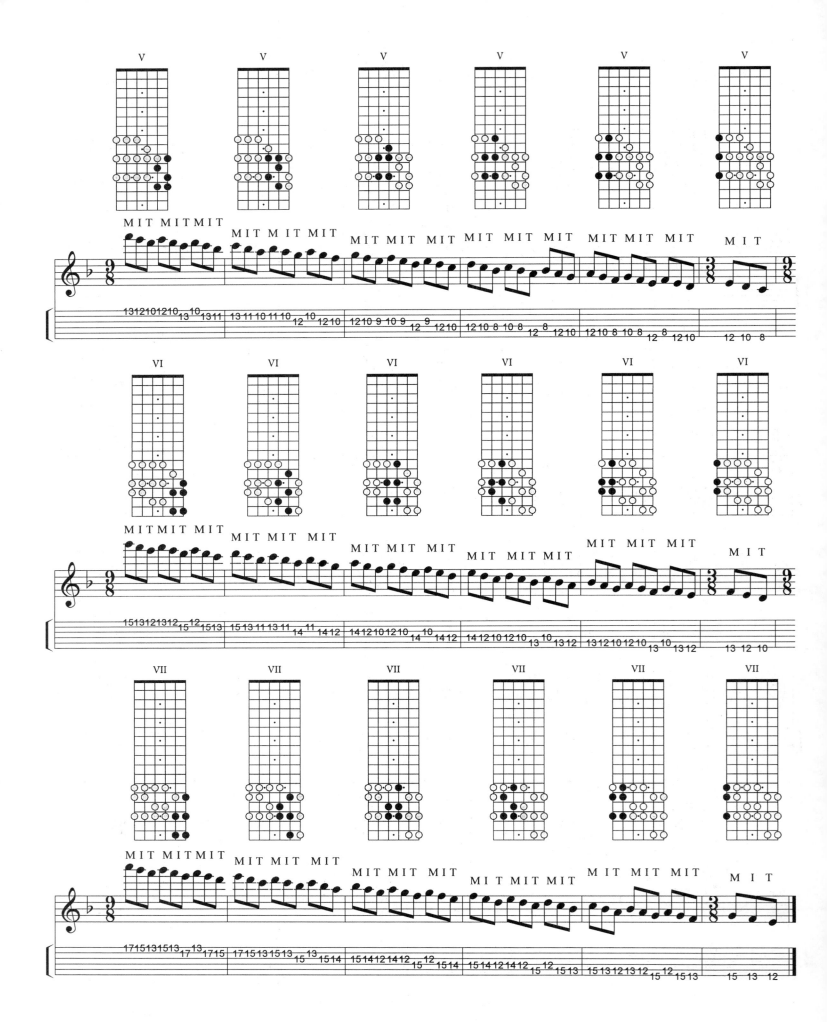

56

THREE NOTE COILS IN F MAJOR (ascending & descending)

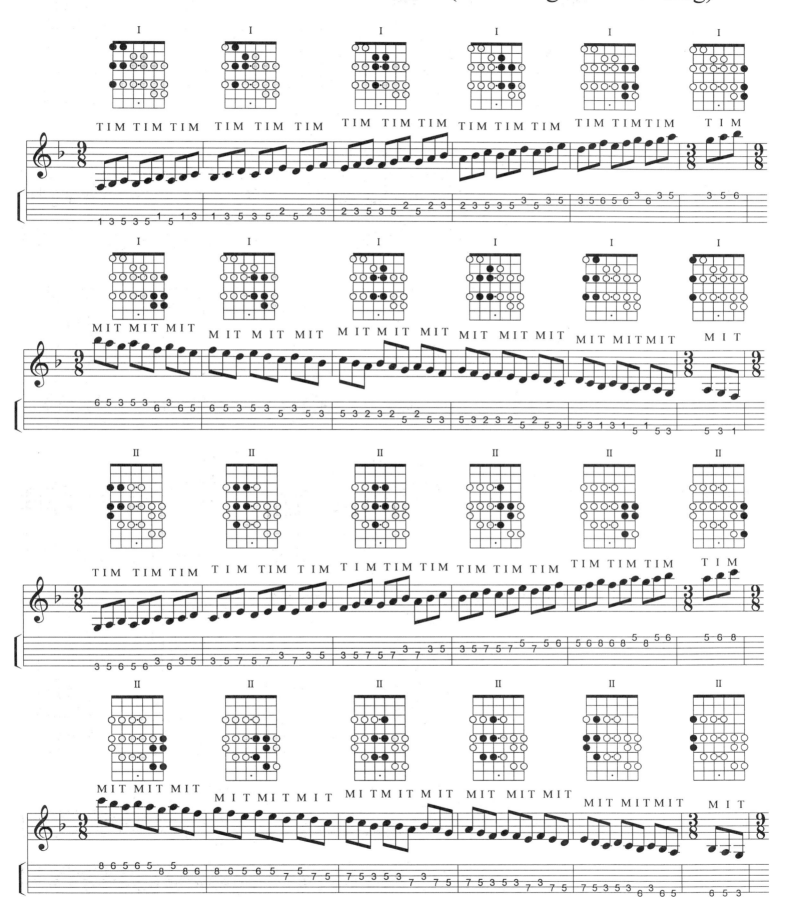

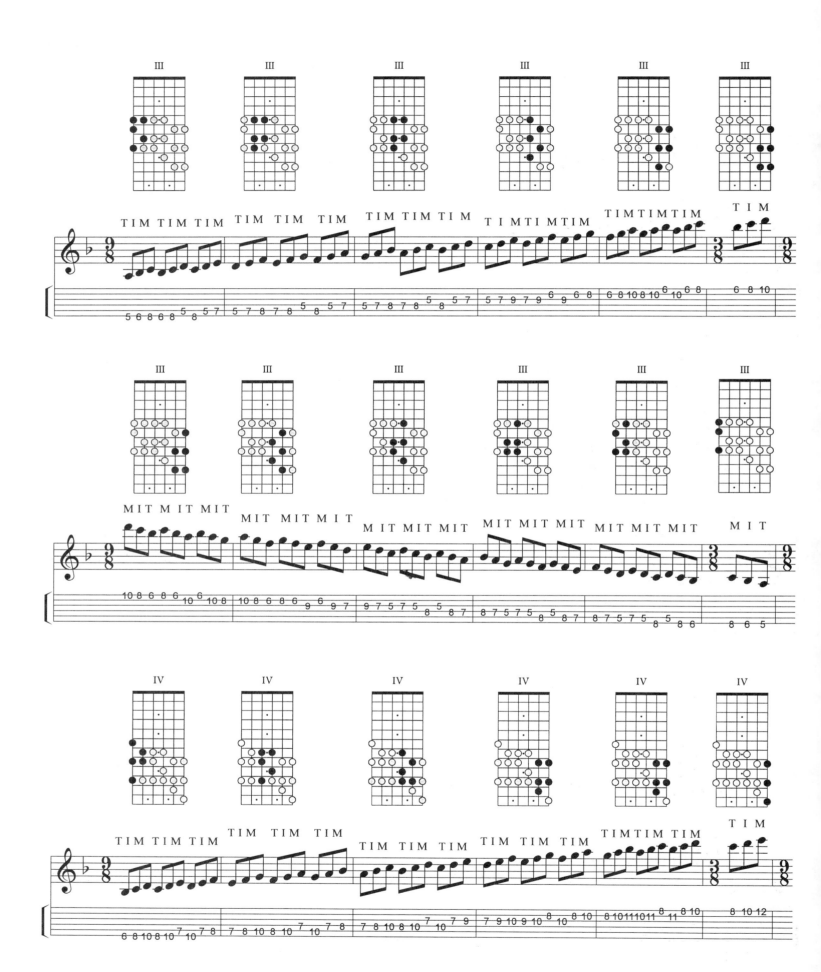

58

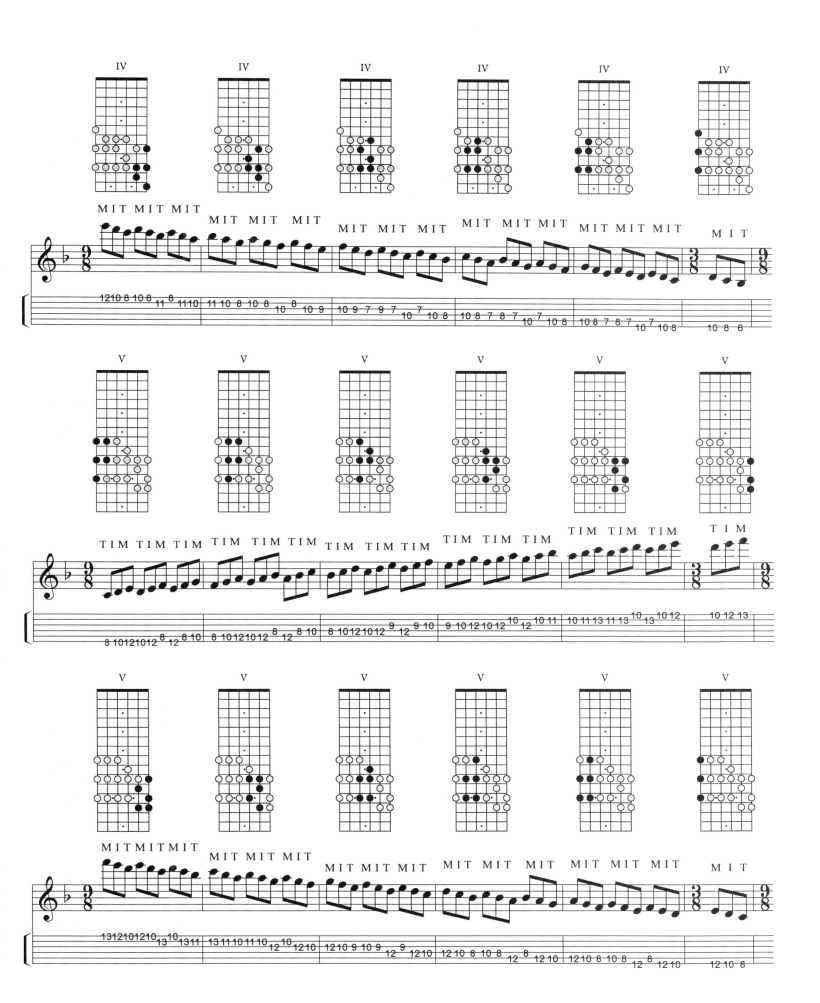

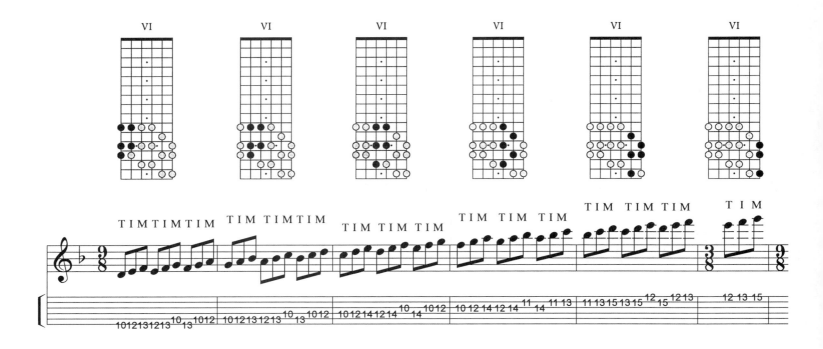

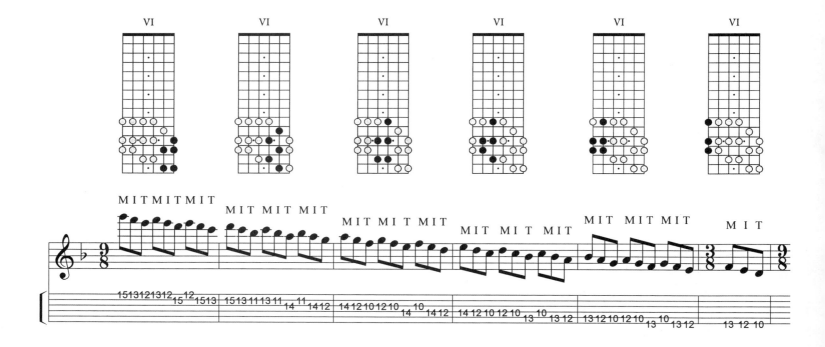

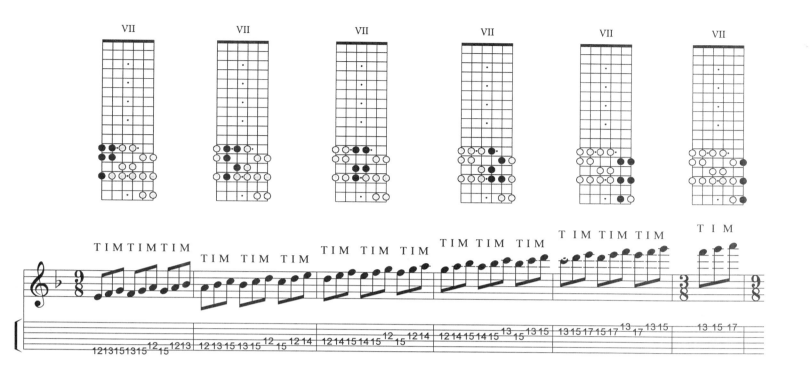

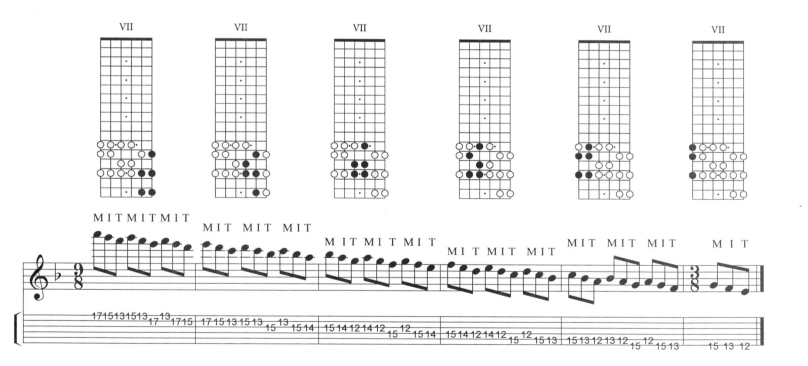

THREE NOTE COILS IN F MAJOR
(ascending & descending - alternating patterns)

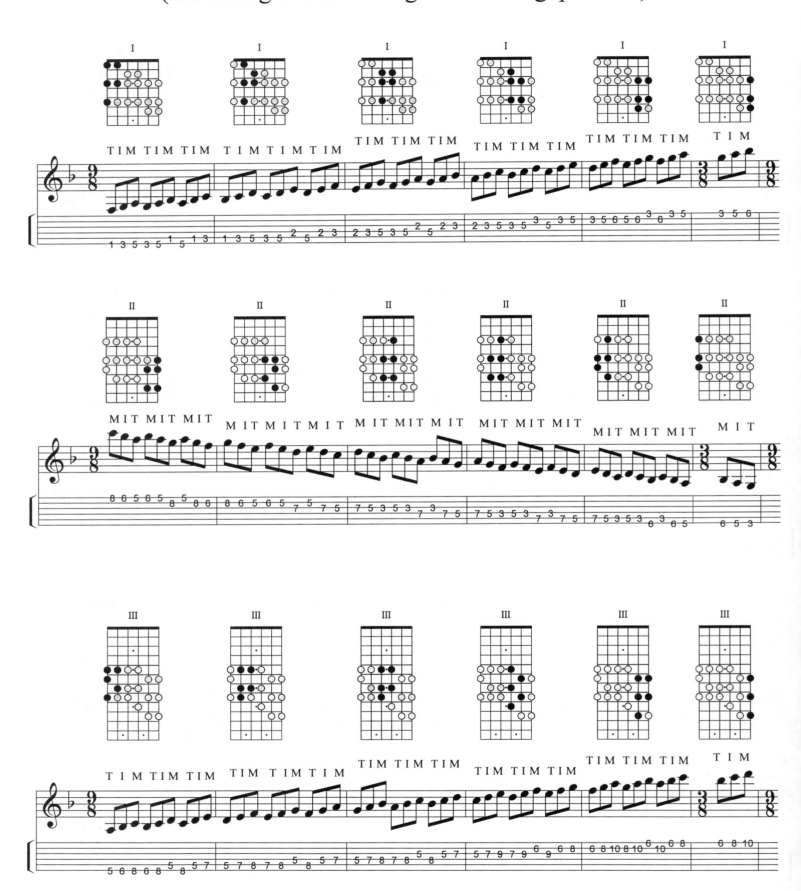

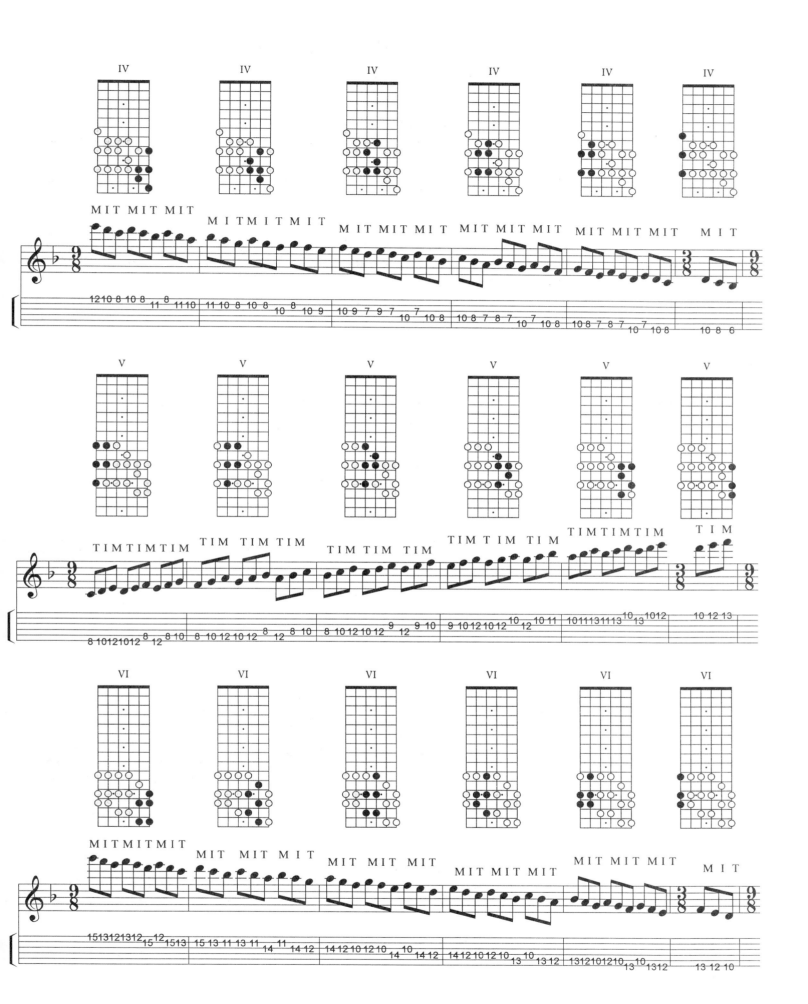

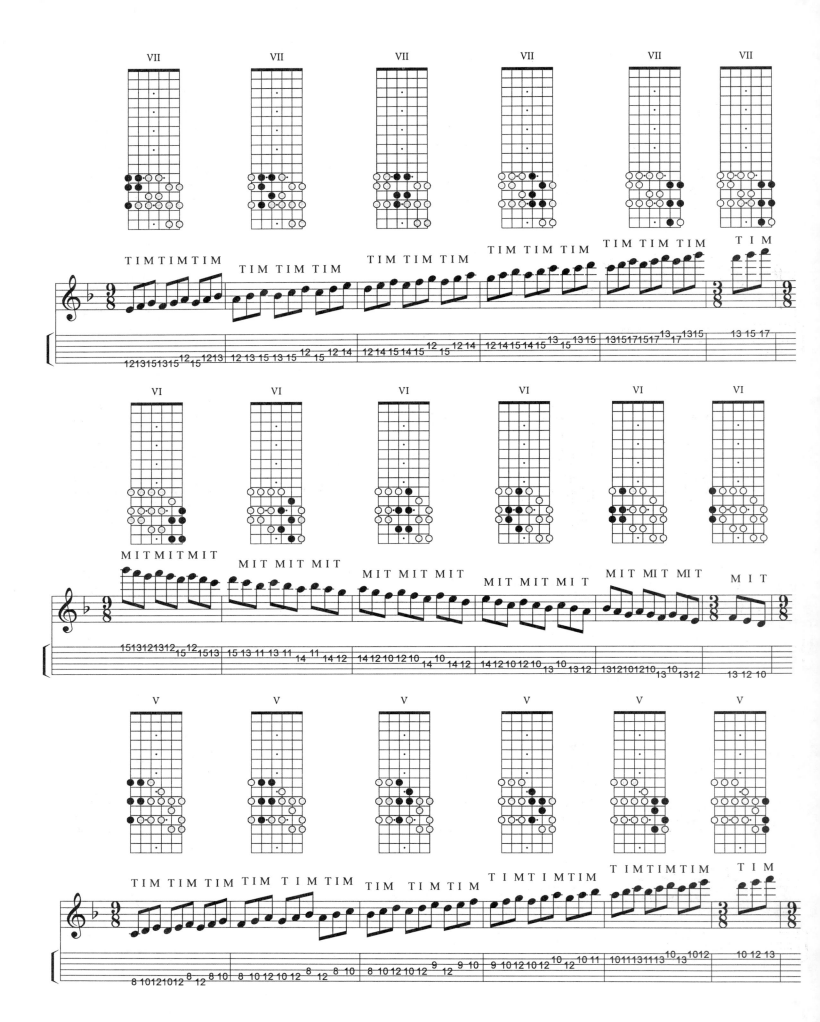

64

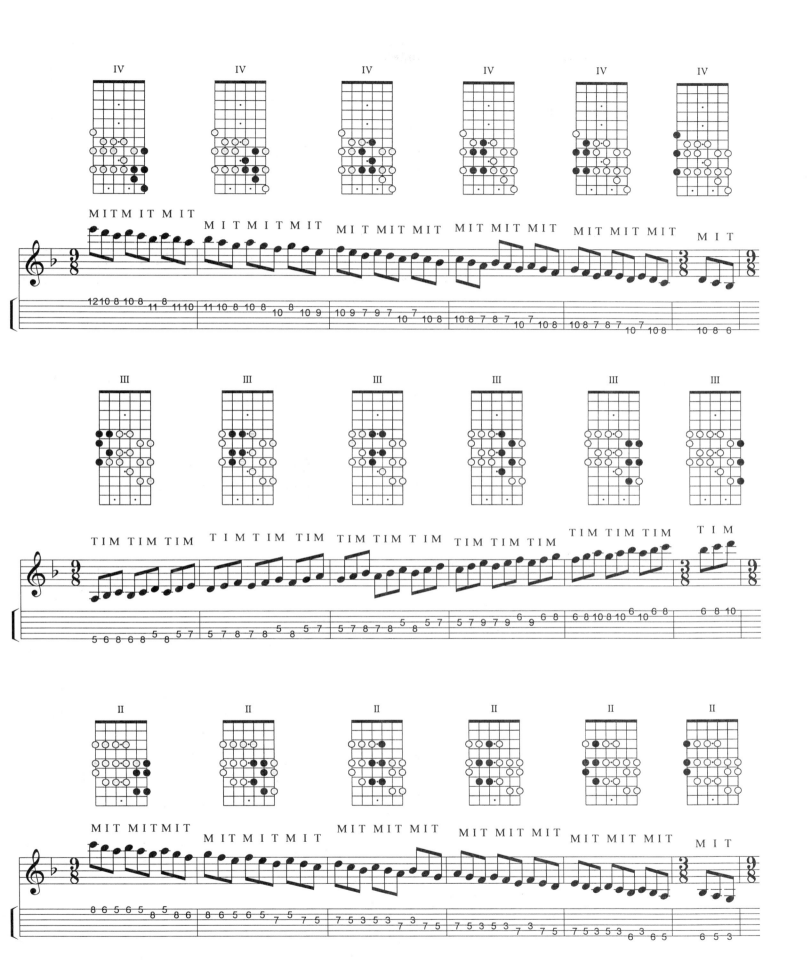

65

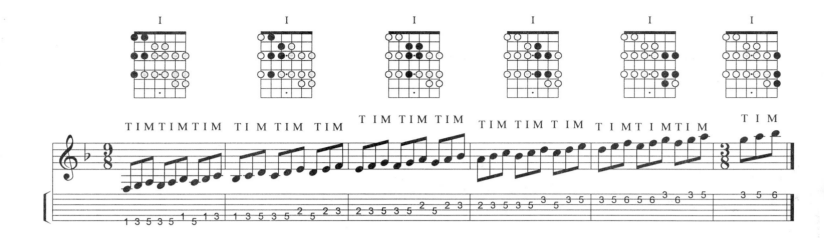

FOUR NOTE COIL ASCENDING PICKING PATTERNS

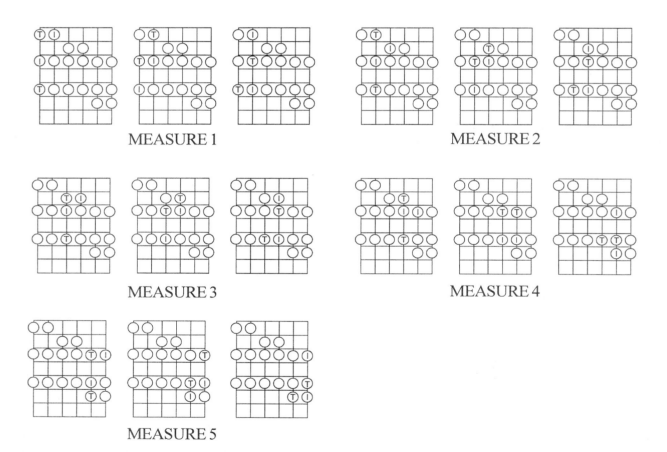

MEASURE 1   MEASURE 2

MEASURE 3   MEASURE 4

MEASURE 5

The same approach is used for the four note coils as in the three note coils. The only difference is you have four note groups rather than three note groups. The right hand fingering of T,I,T,I can also be replaced with T,I,M,R or I,M,I,M for the sake of exercising the fingers. It is a good idea to alternate between the three different fingerings for dexterity practice.

FOUR NOTE COILS IN F MAJOR (ascending)

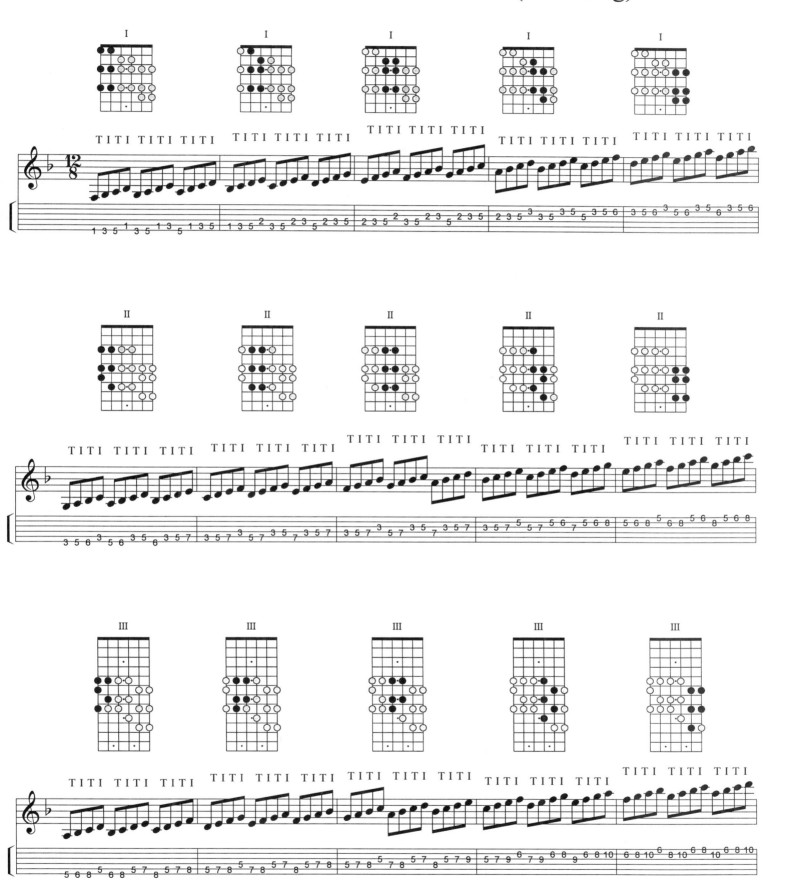

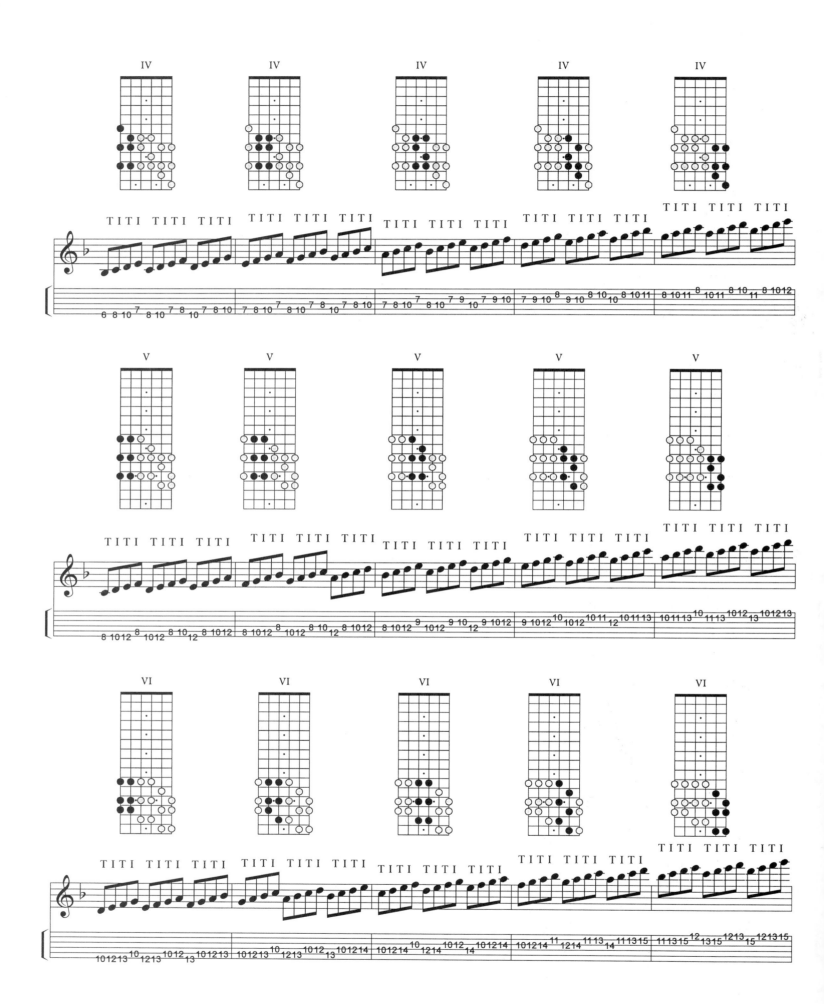

68

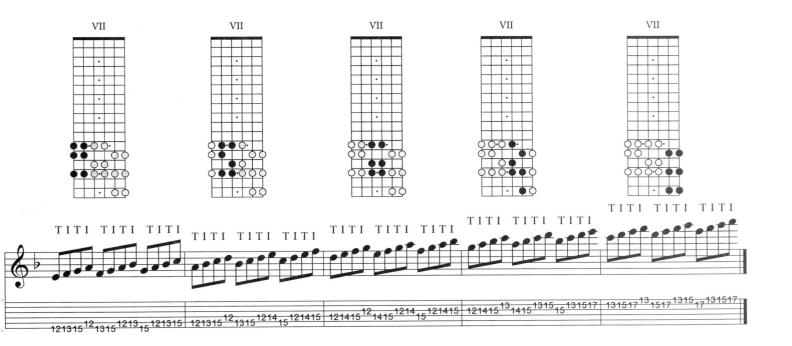

FOUR NOTE COIL DESCENDING PICKING PATTERNS

By now you should be familiar with this. So here is the breakdown of the fingerpicking pattern for the four note coils.

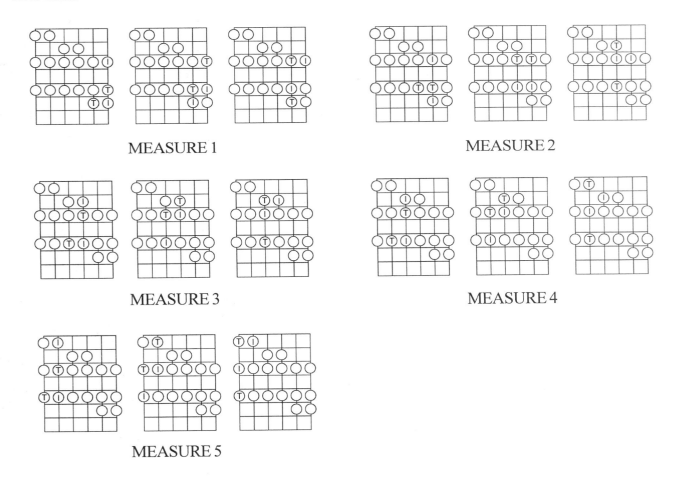

MEASURE 1   MEASURE 2

MEASURE 3   MEASURE 4

MEASURE 5

69

FOUR NOTE COILS IN F MAJOR (descending)

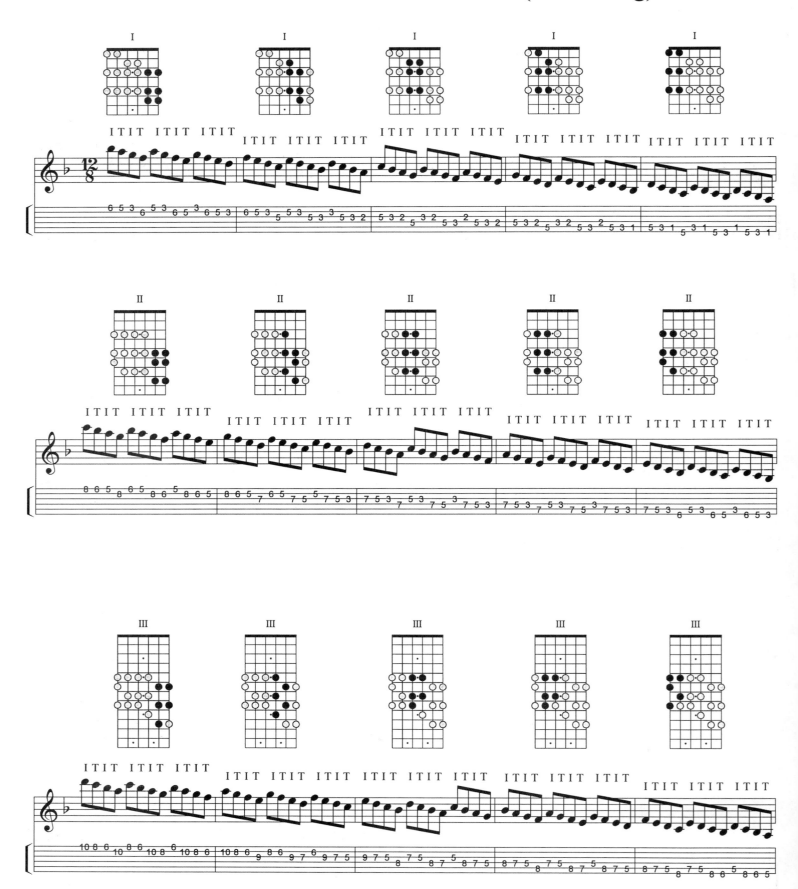

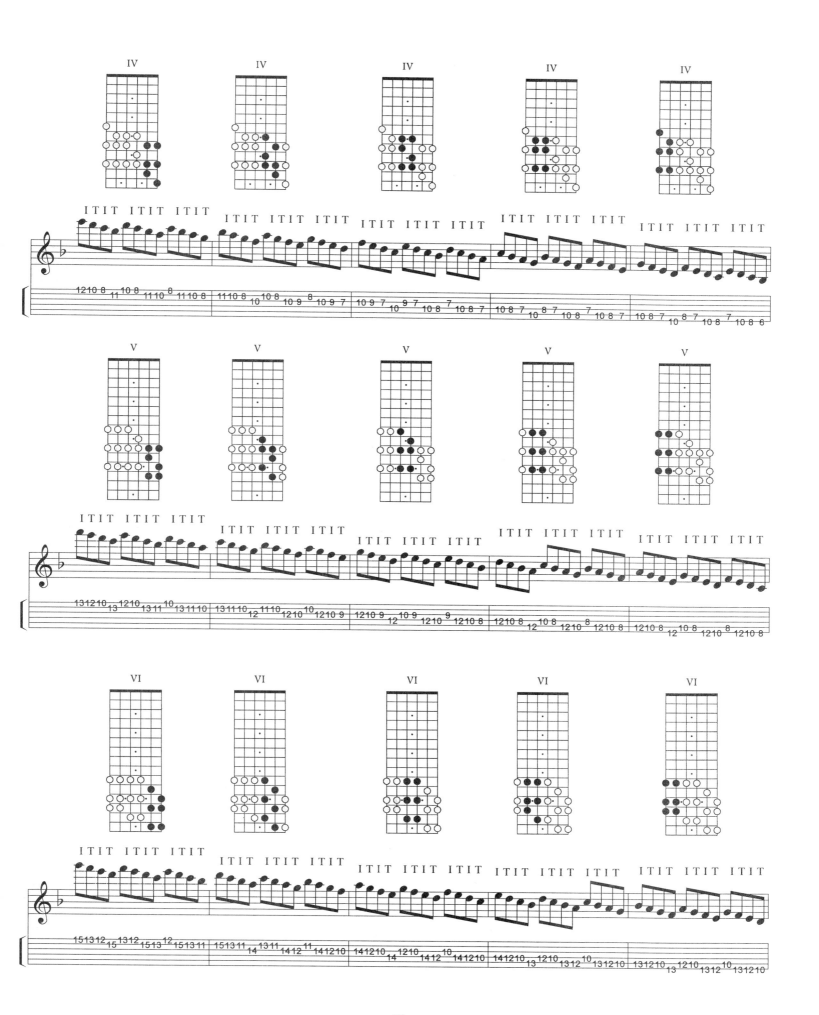

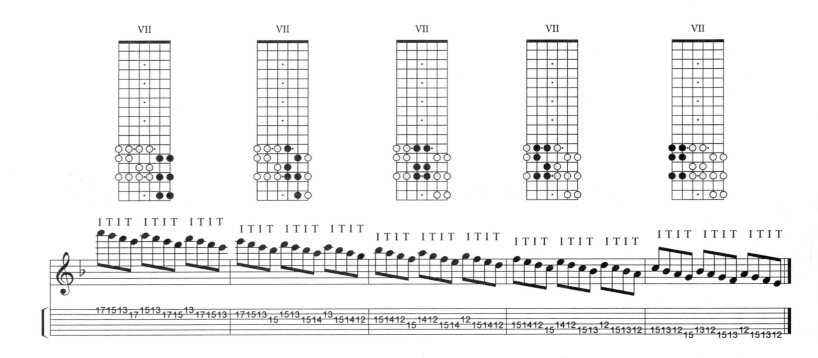

Now we will put the two together for ascending and descending with four note coils.

FOUR NOTE COILS IN F MAJOR (ascending & descending)

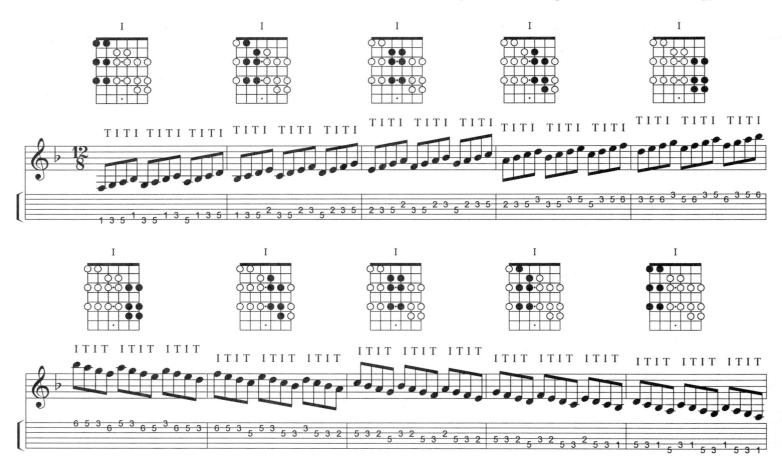

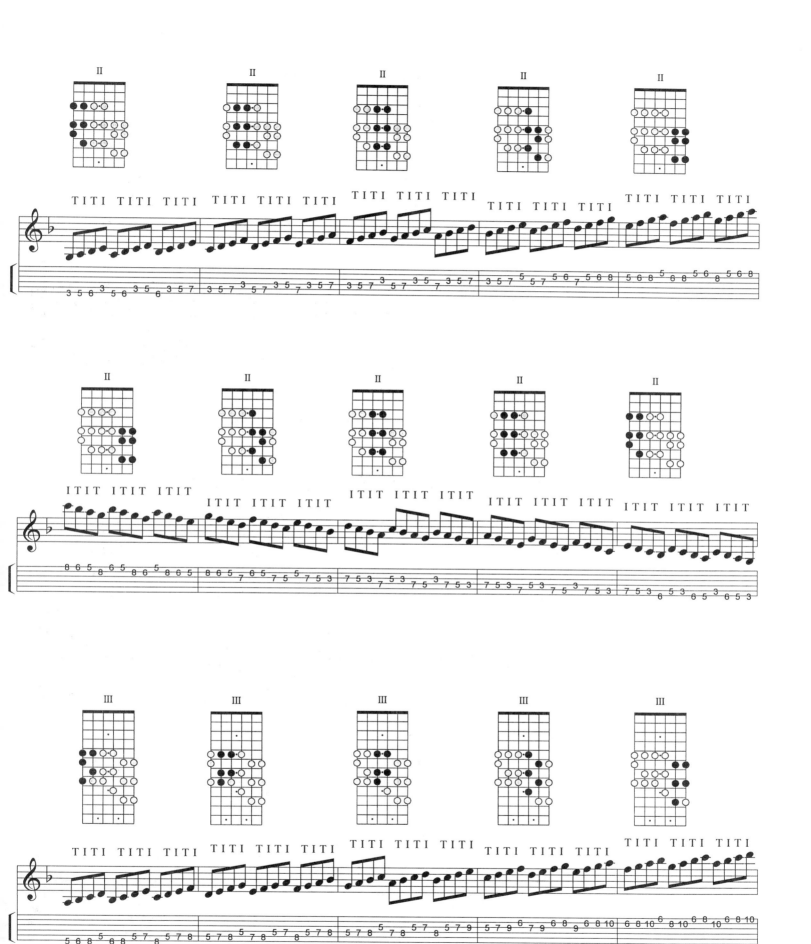

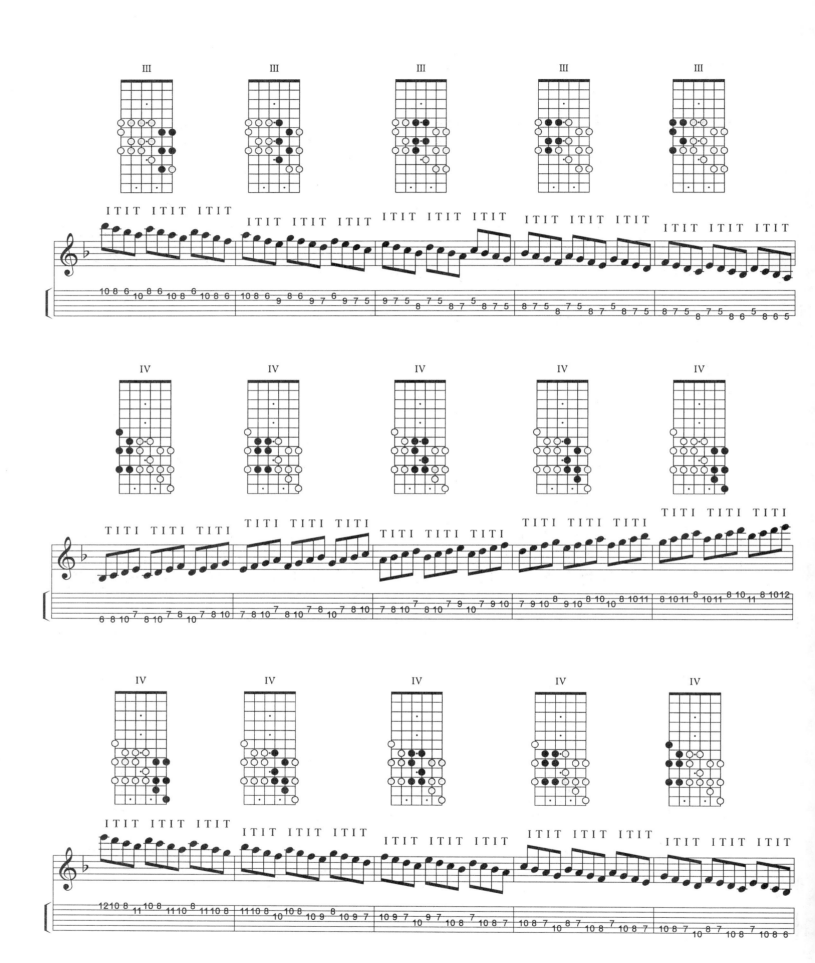

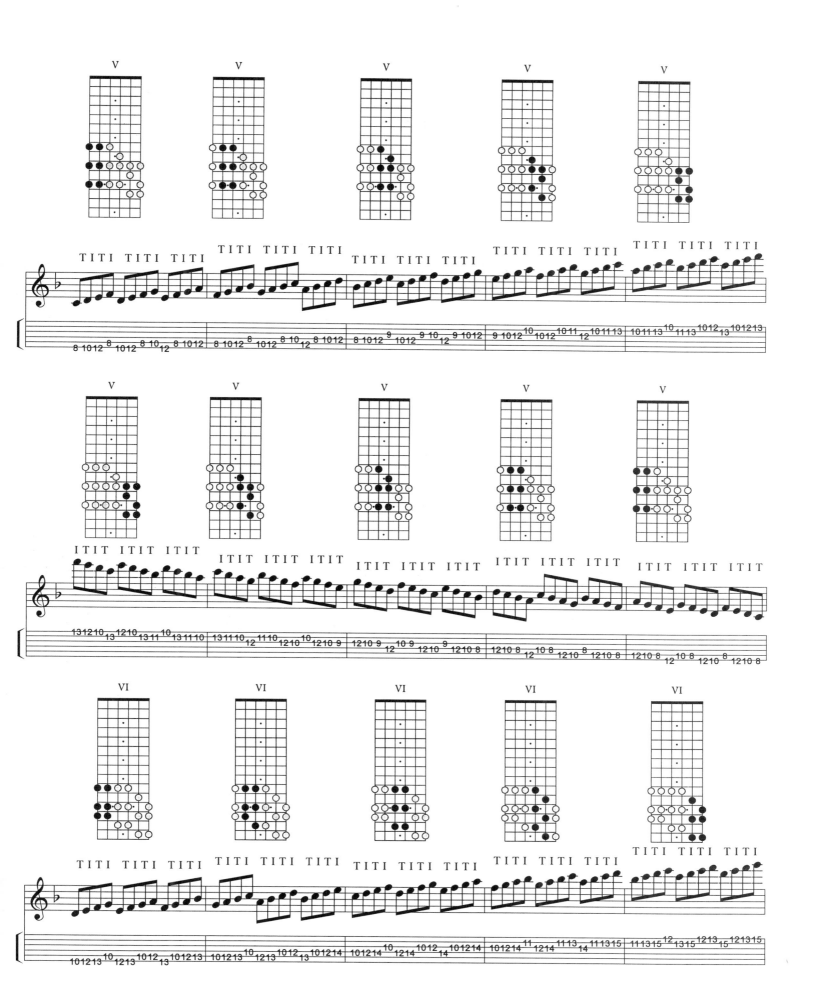

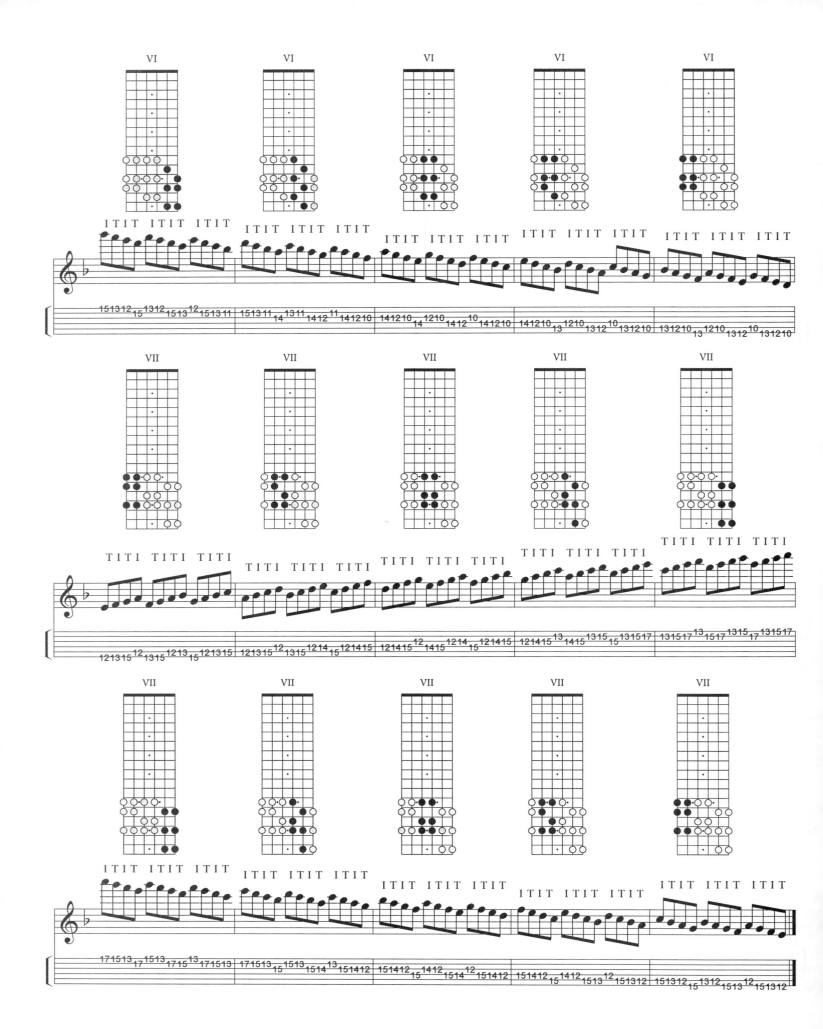

76

FOUR NOTE COILS IN F MAJOR
(ascending & descending - alternating patterns)

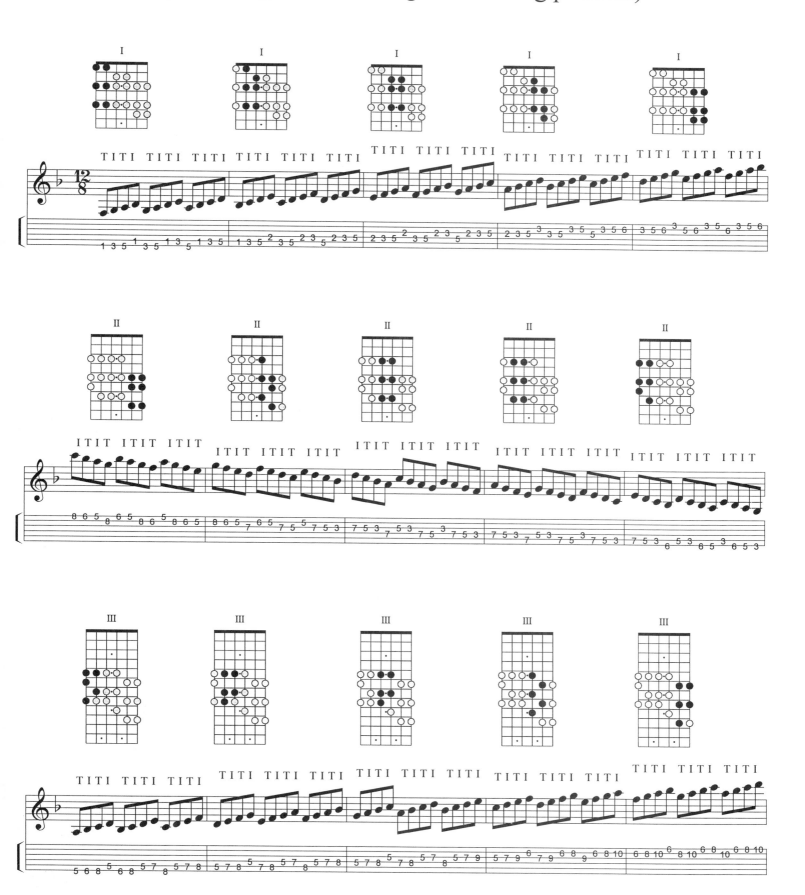

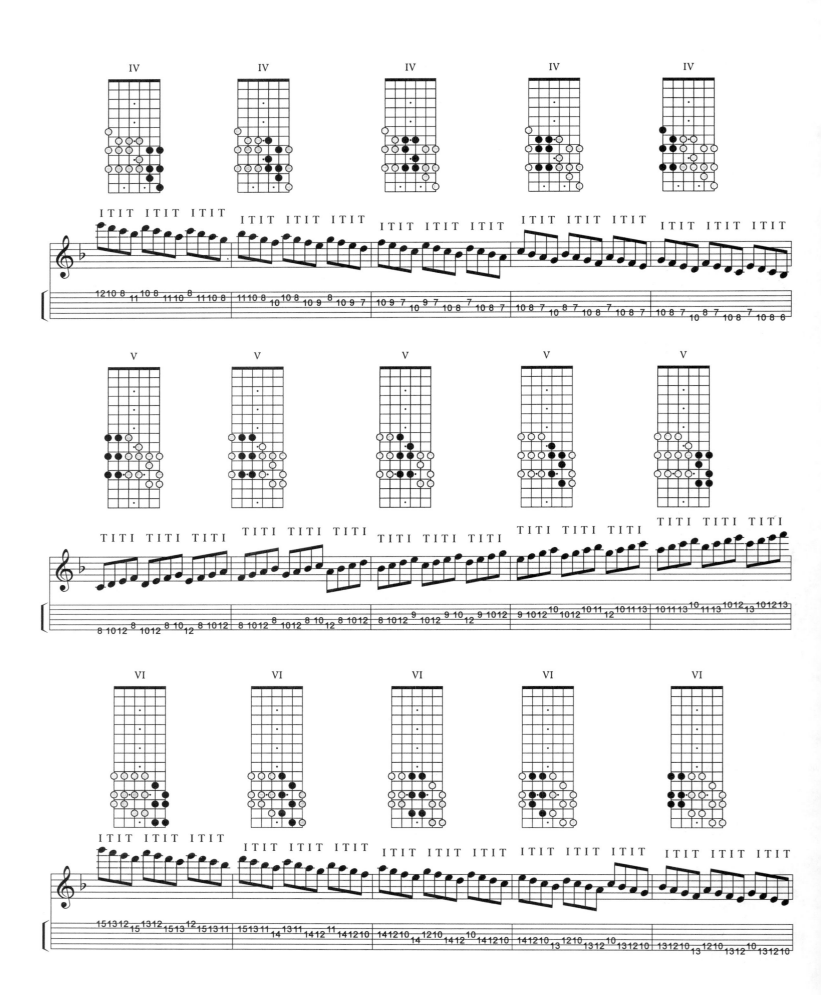

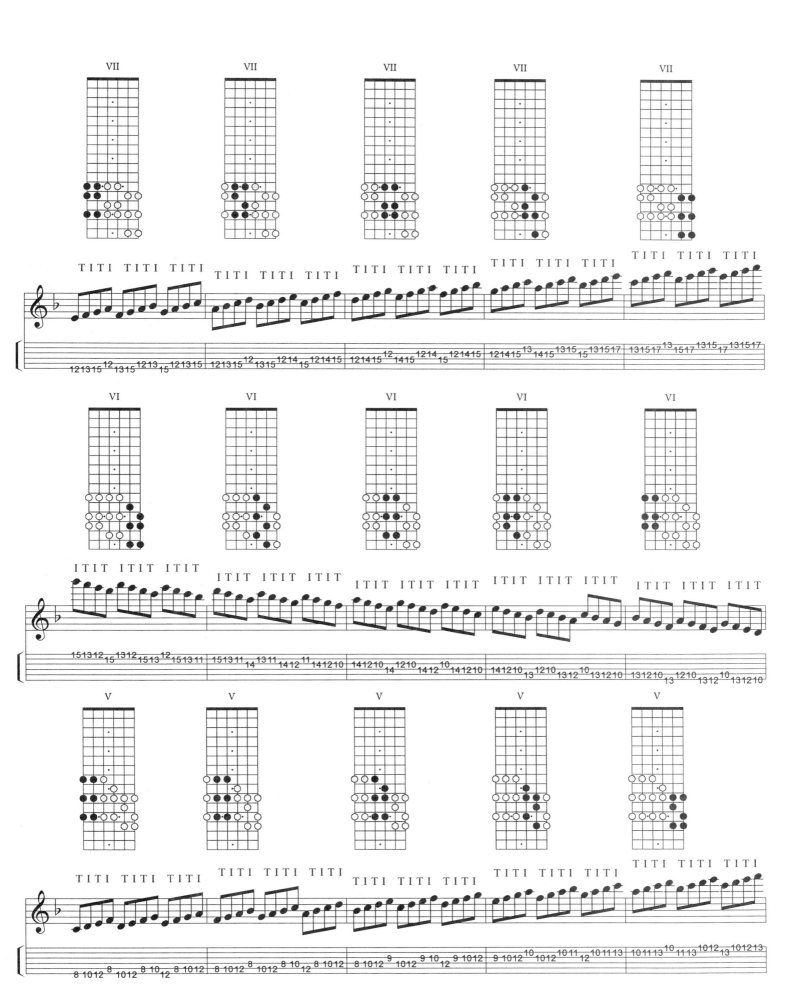

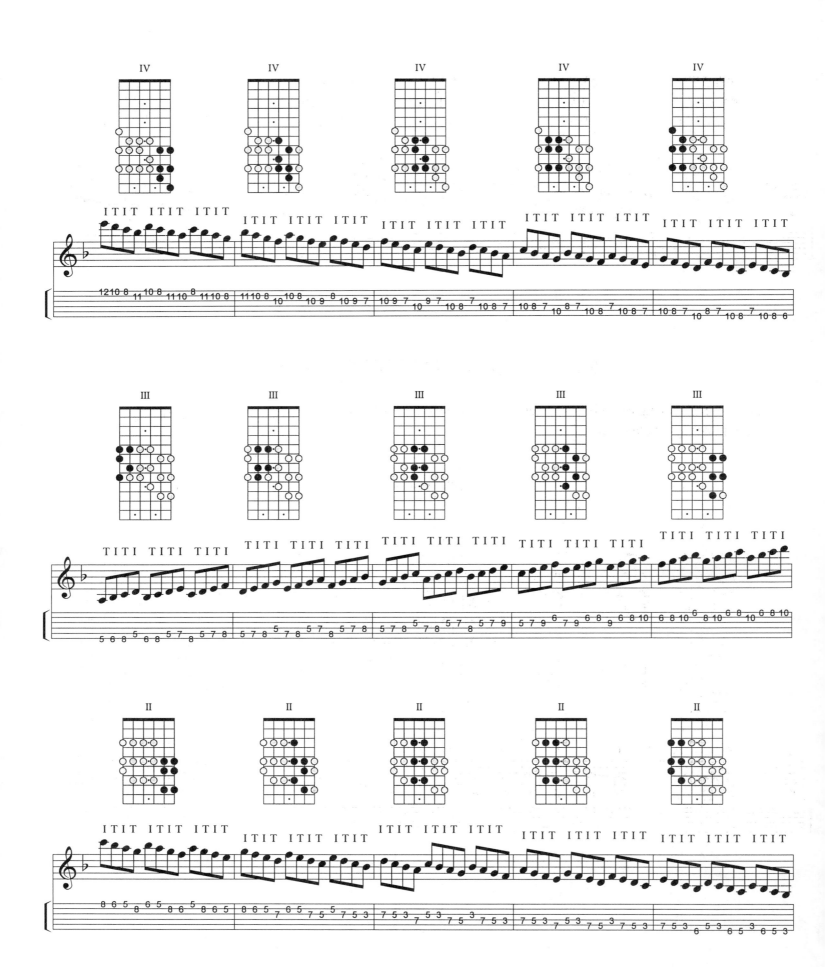

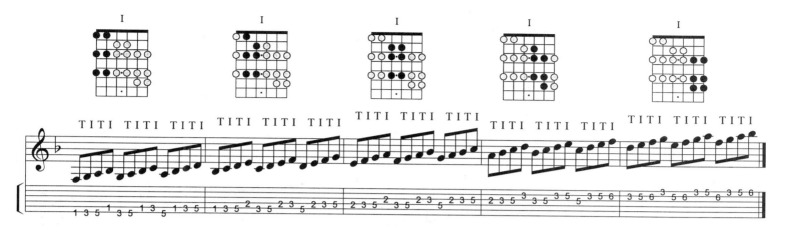

SINGLE STRING EXERCISES

These single string exercises are designed to give the ability to change patterns from any string. The fingerpicking pattern is T,I,M.

6th String

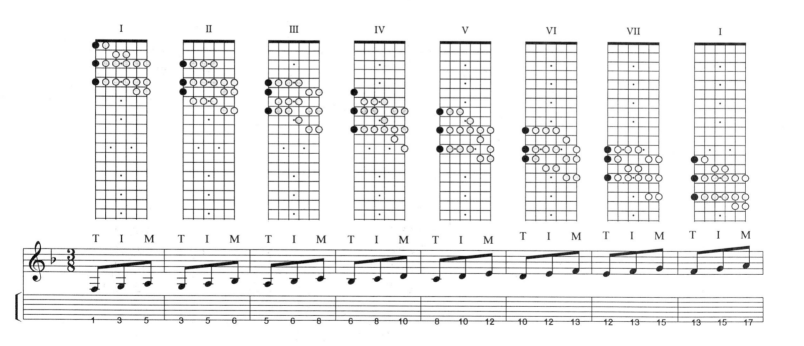

5th String

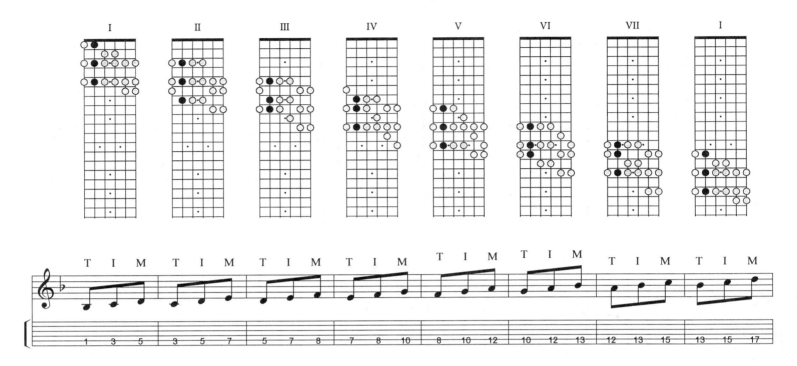

4th String

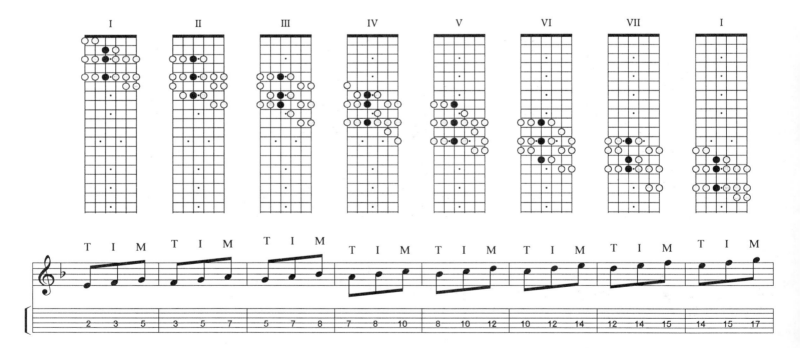

82

3rd String

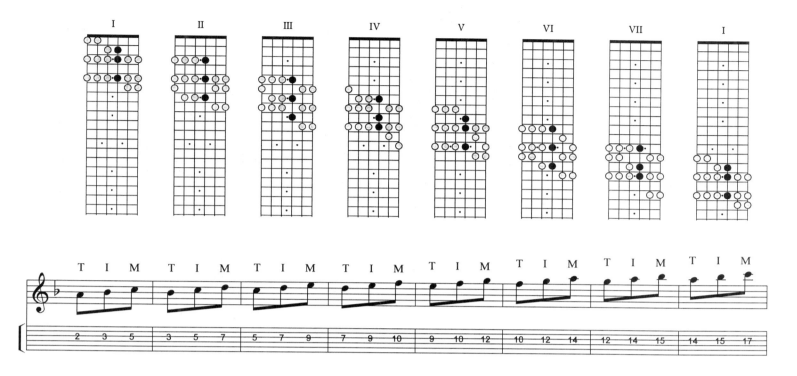

2nd String

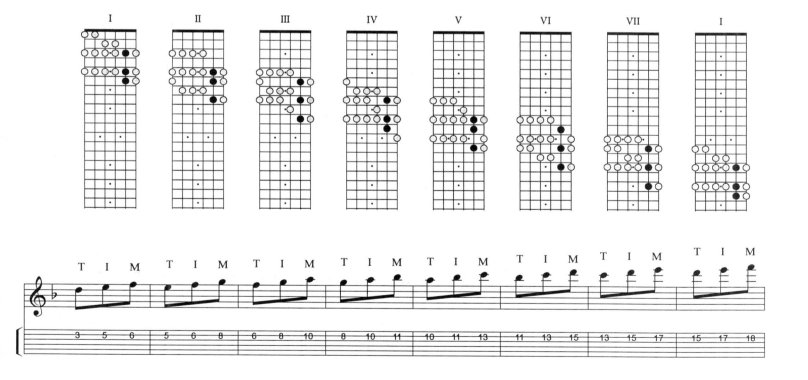

1st String

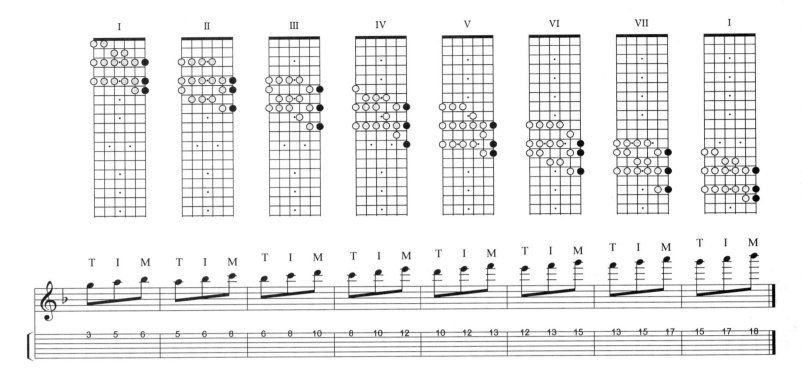

TWO STRING EXERCISES

This next bunch is two string exercises. They're also designed to develop inner pattern changing using two strings. After you learn these you can then do them in groups of five (quintuplets) or groups of six (sextuplets).

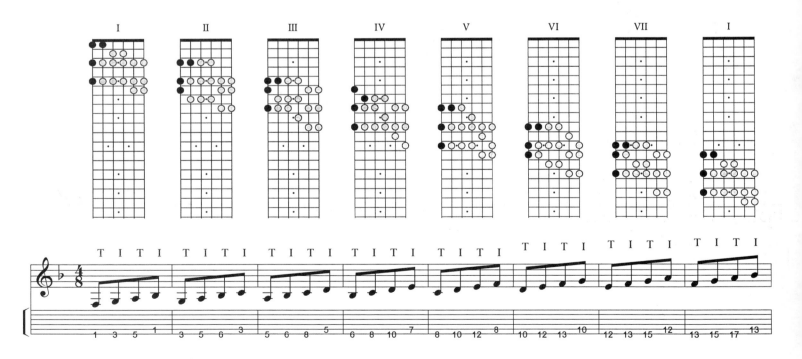

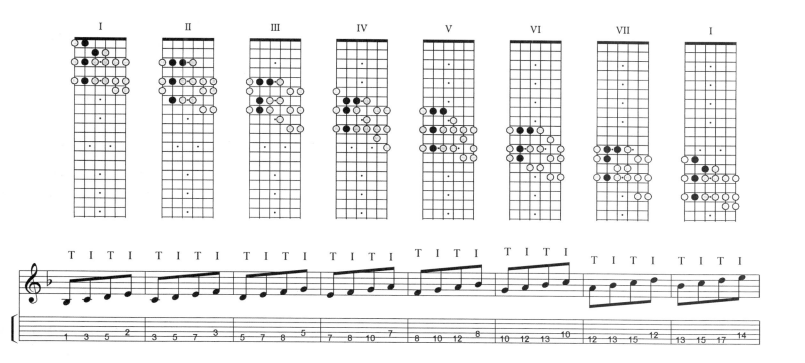

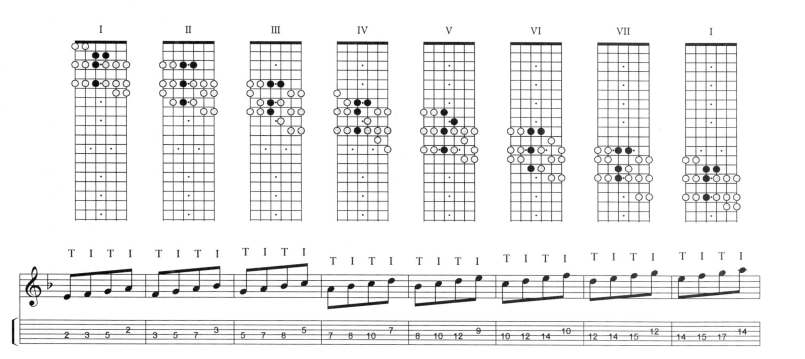

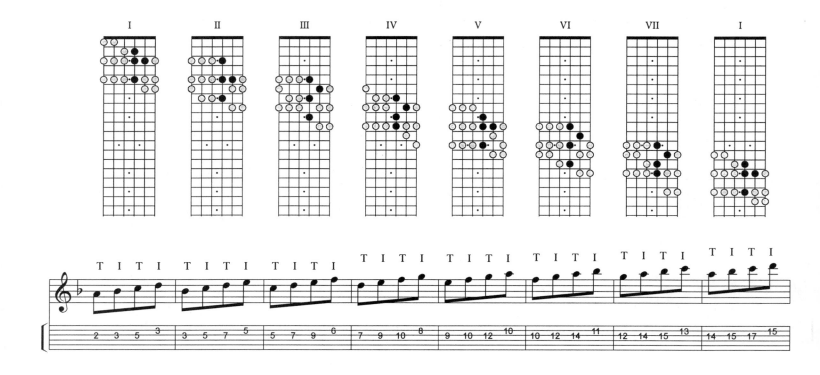

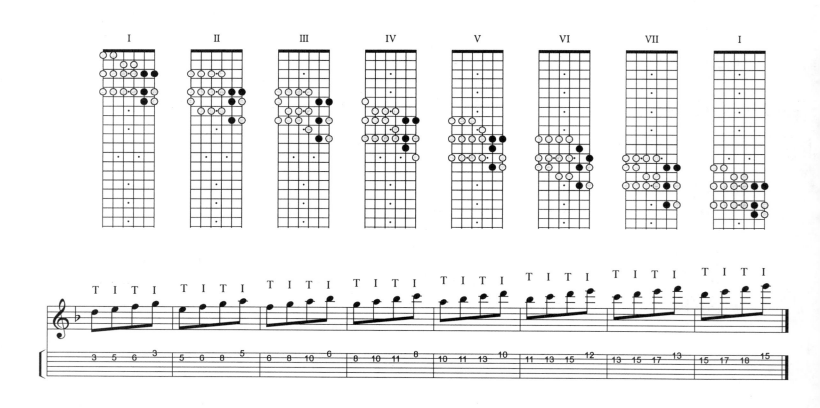

SCALE TONE THIRDS IN F MAJOR (ascending)

The next exercise is scale tone thirds. The reason it is called scale tone thirds is that you are using every other note of the scale, in this case the Major scale in F. By doing so some of the thirds are minor thirds as well as major thirds. If you used straight major thirds the whole time you would be using the whole-tone scale.

The fingerpicking pattern for this one remains a constant T,I, T,I, T,I. You can also practice the patterns with I,T.

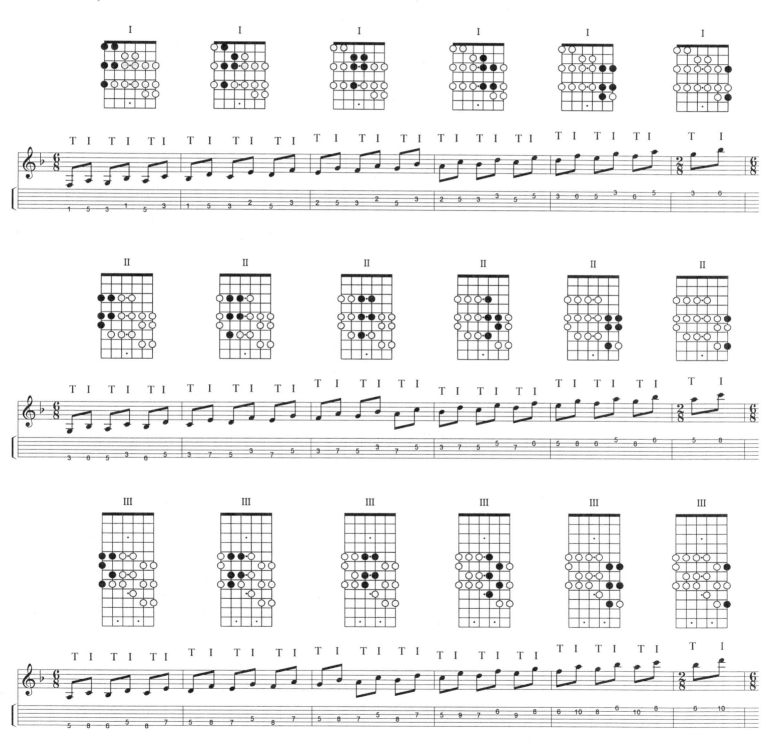

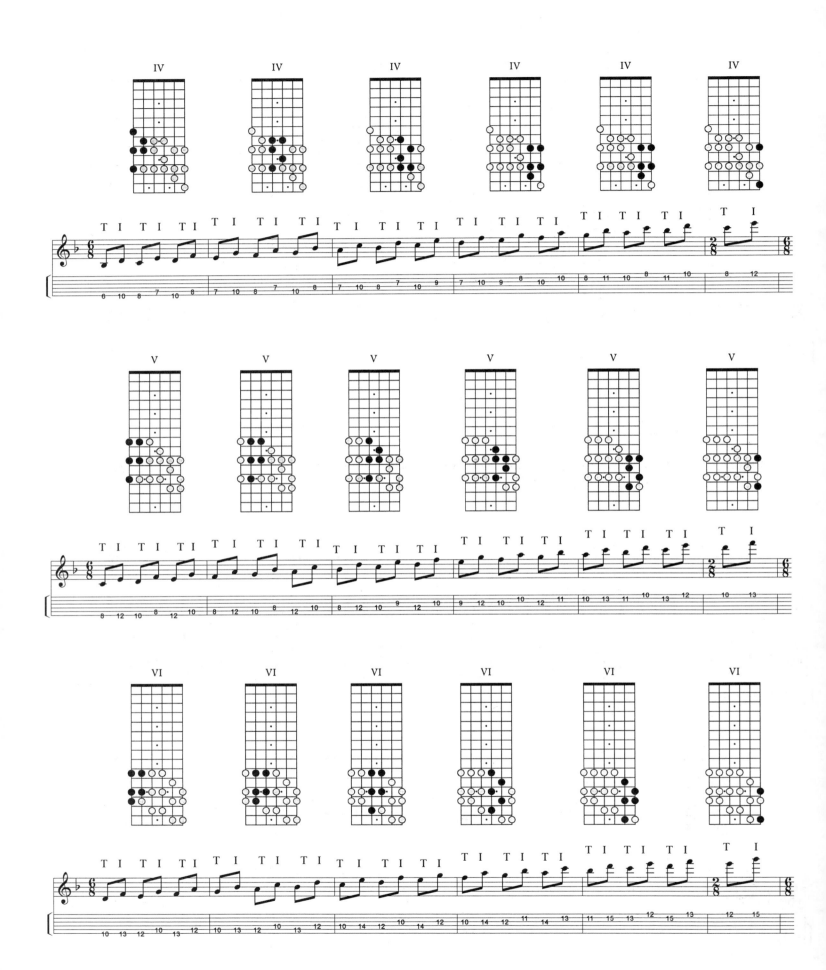

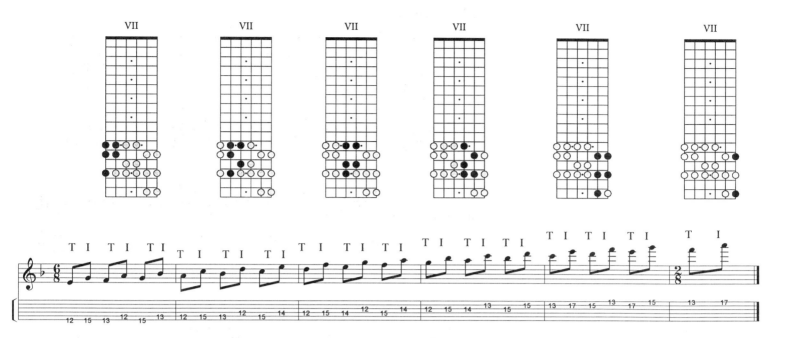

SCALE TONE THIRDS IN F MAJOR (descending)

Now we learn the same thing descending. The fingerpicking pattern to descend is also T,I, T,I, T,I. You can also practice the patterns using I,T.

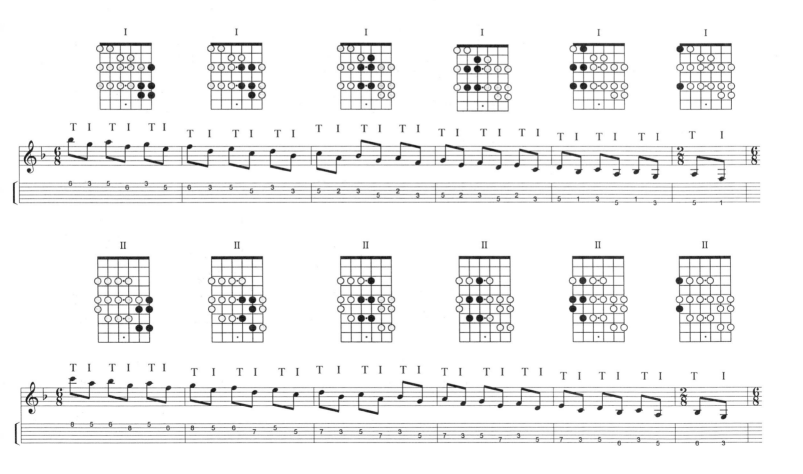

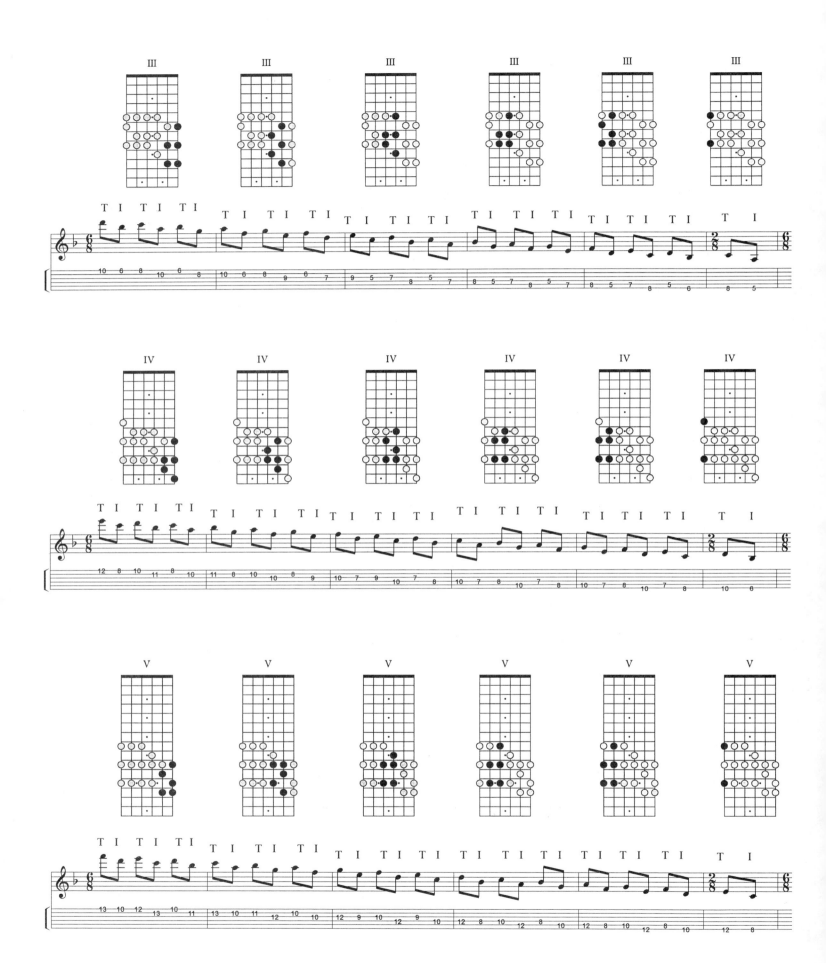

90

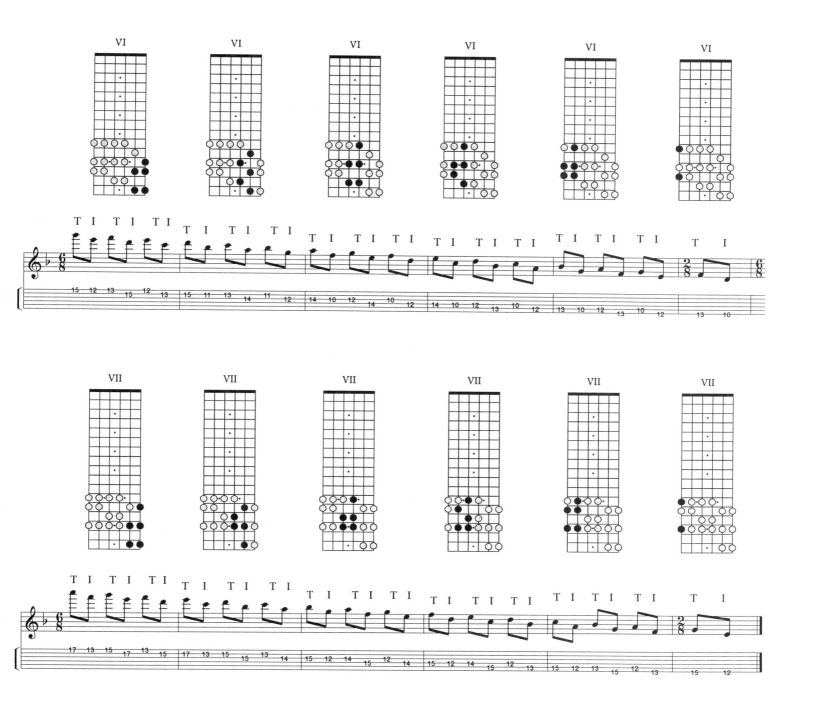

SCALE TONE THIRDS IN F MAJOR
(ascending & descending)

Now we put the two together ascending and descending.

91

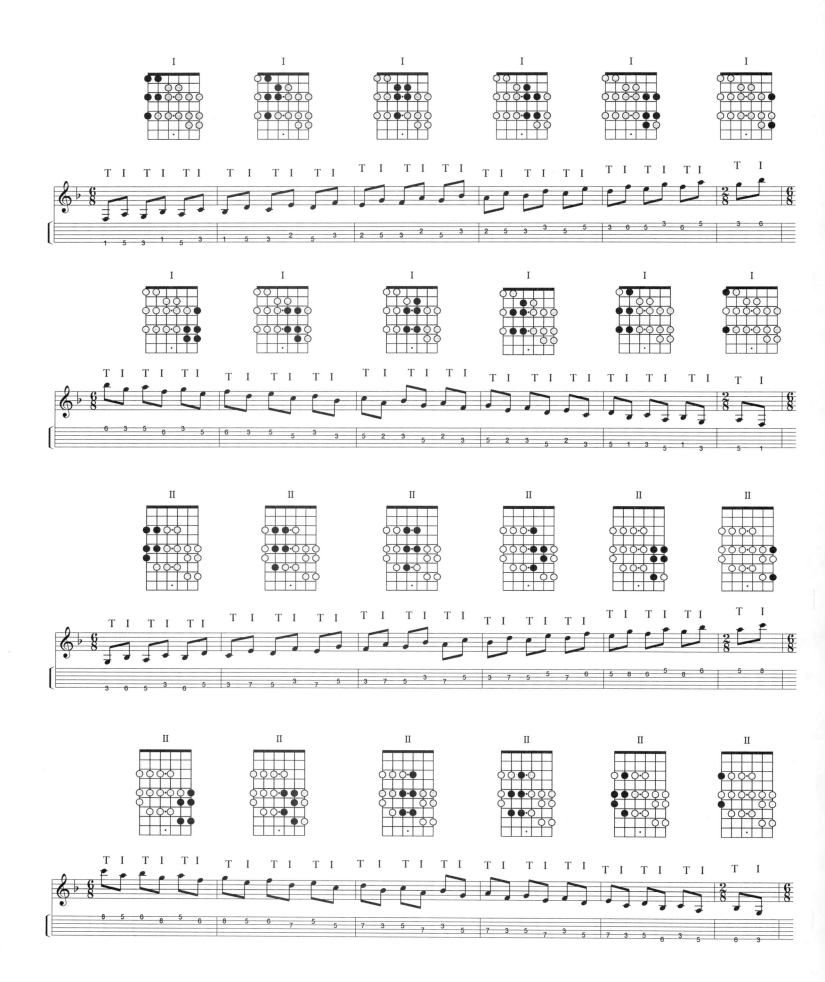

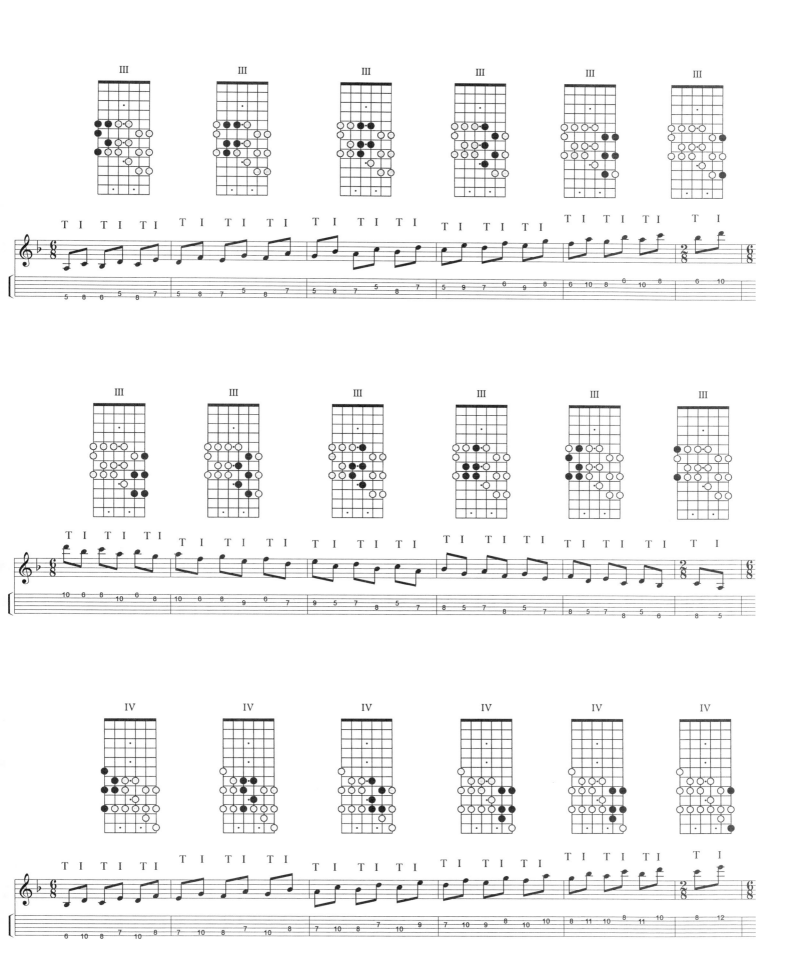

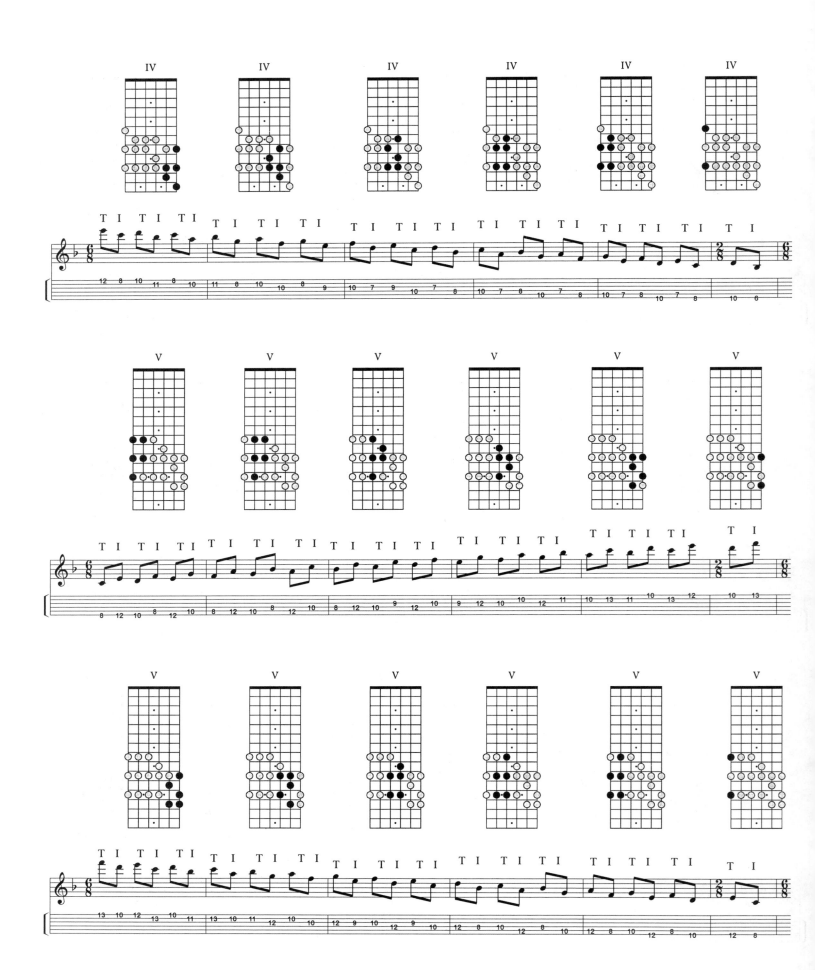

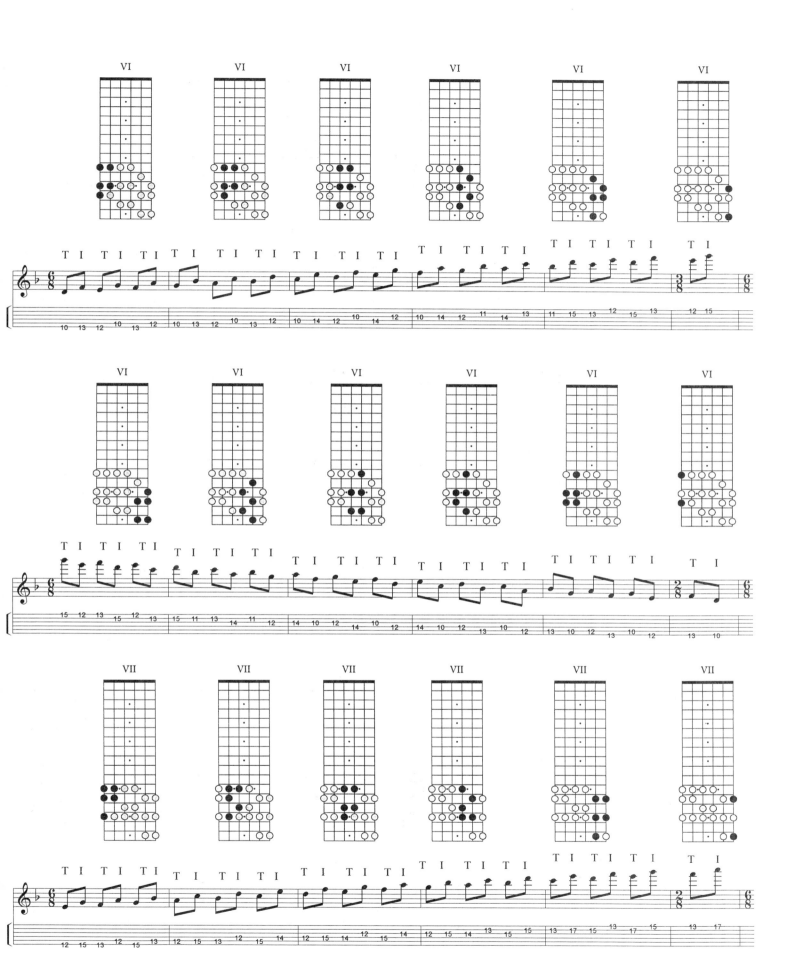

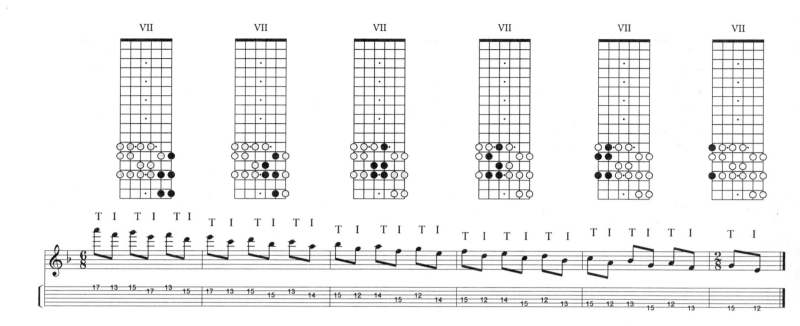

SCALE TONE THIRDS IN F MAJOR
(ascending & descending - alternating)

Now we ascend and descend while alternating the patterns. The picking pattern down, up, down, up remains the same.

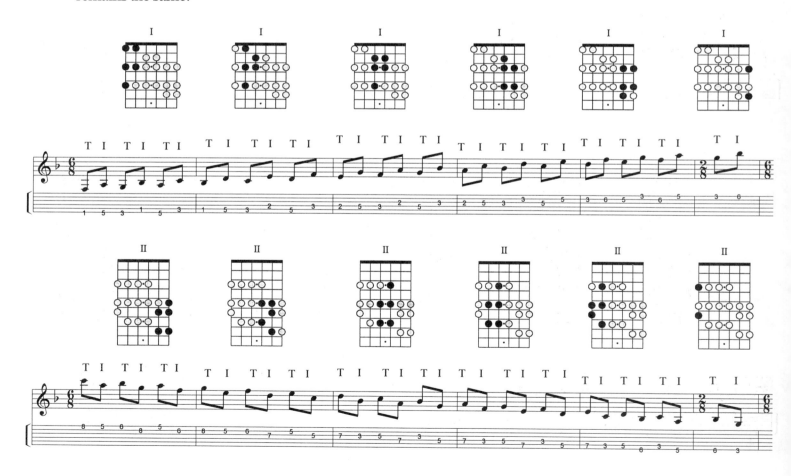

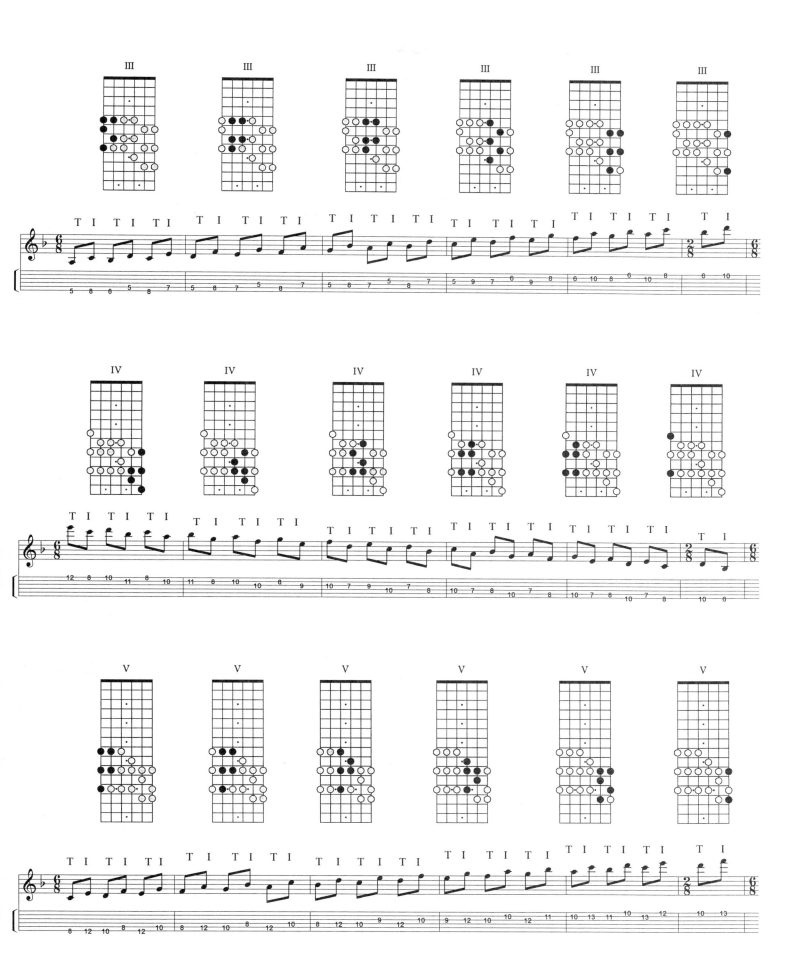

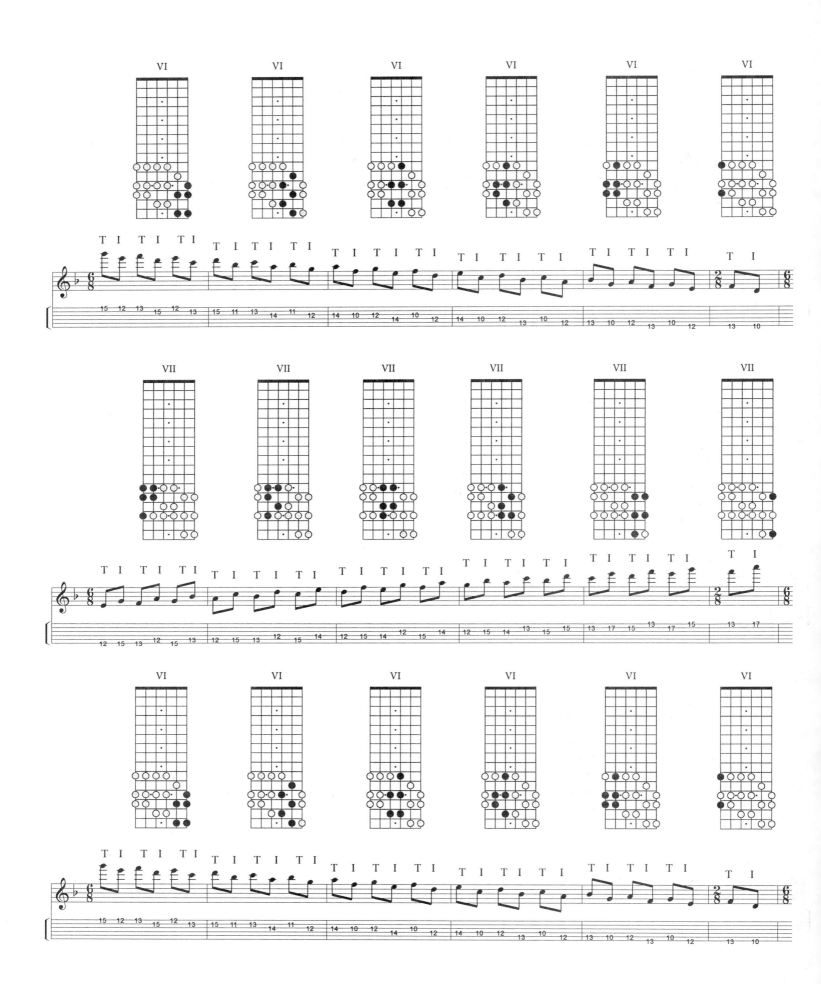

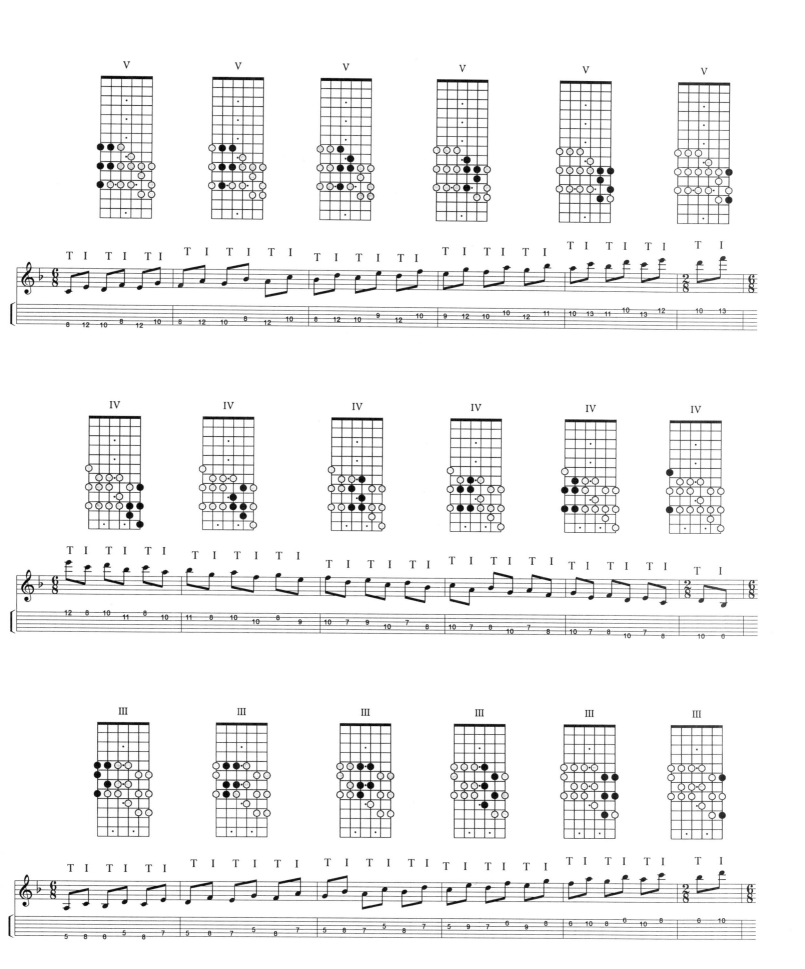

99

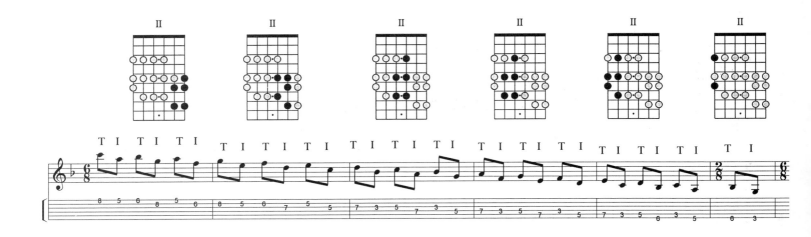

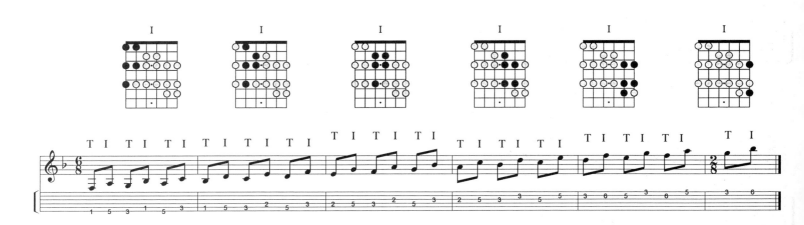

The following pages show the patterns in all the other keys. Every exercise you have learned in F will work in all the keys. Now you will see what I was talking about earlier on page 41 that the other keys don't start with pattern 1.

F# MAJOR

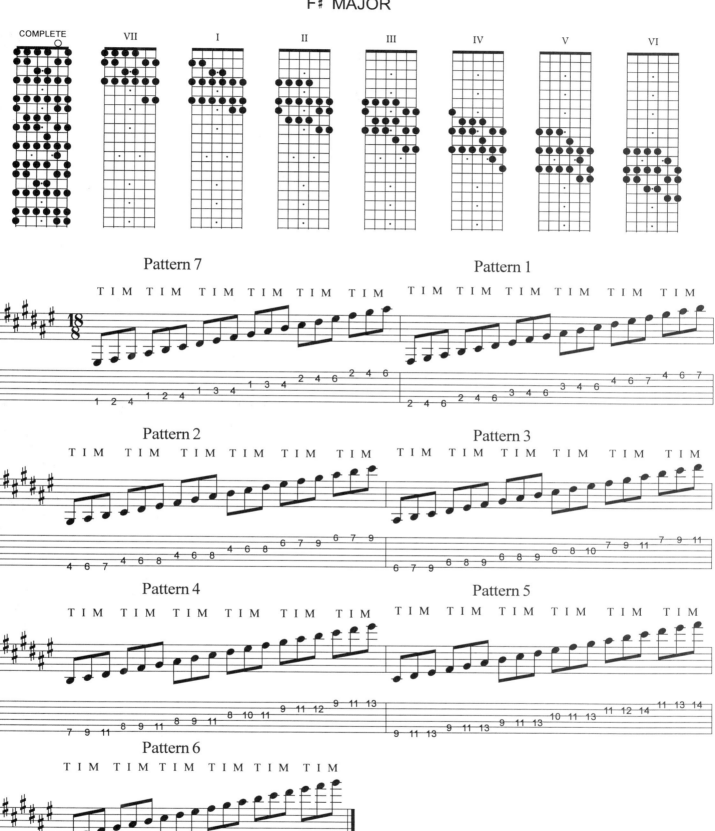

G♭ MAJOR

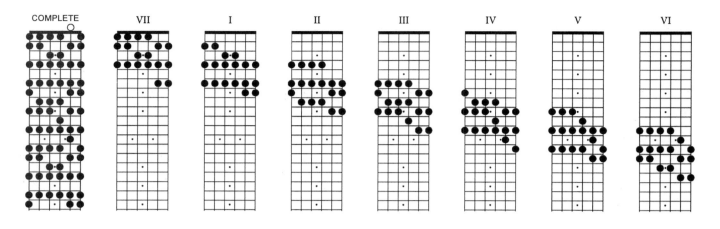

Pattern 7
Pattern 1

Pattern 2
Pattern 3

Pattern 4
Pattern 5
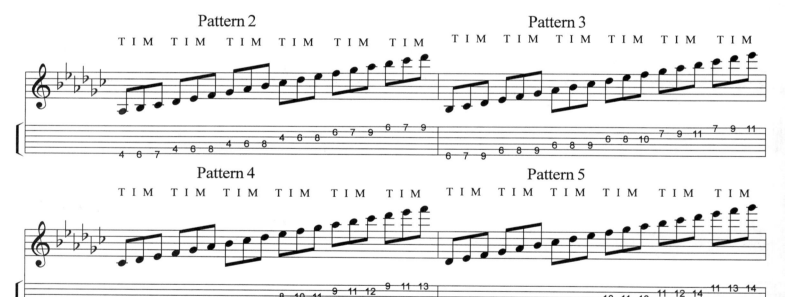

Pattern 6

G♭ Major is the same as F♯ Major. It is included here for the sake of studying the notation.

G MAJOR

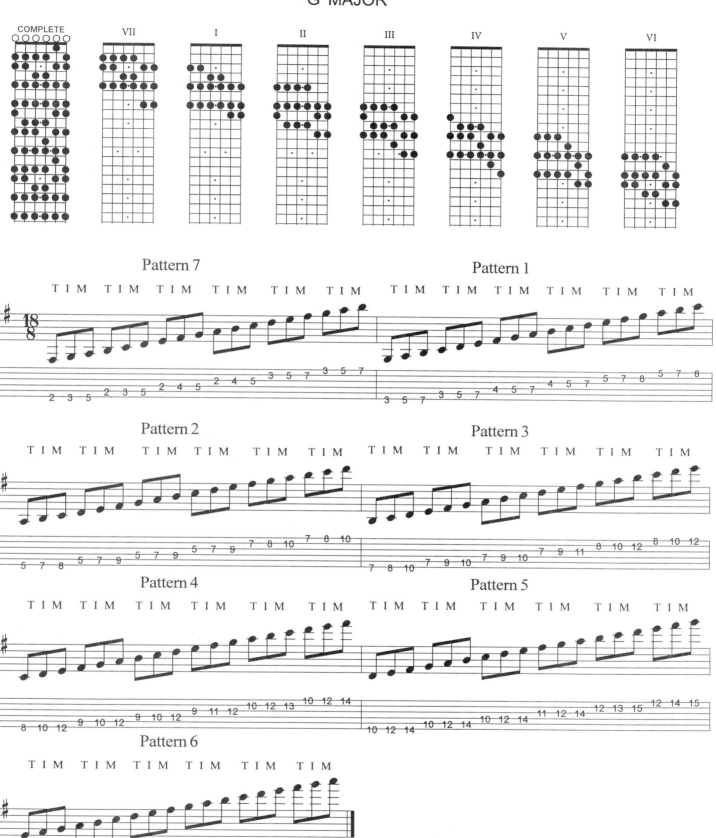

Pattern 7

Pattern 1

Pattern 2

Pattern 3

Pattern 4

Pattern 5

Pattern 6

A♭ MAJOR

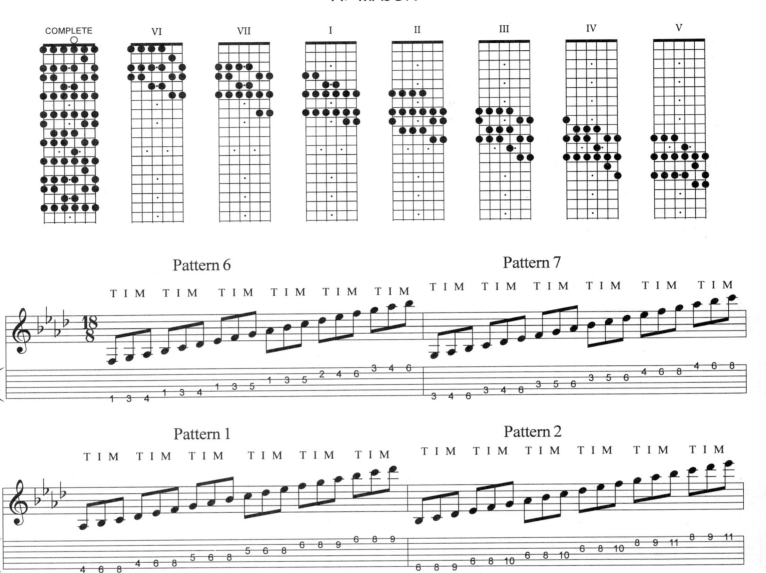

Pattern 6

Pattern 7

Pattern 1

Pattern 2

Pattern 3

Pattern 4

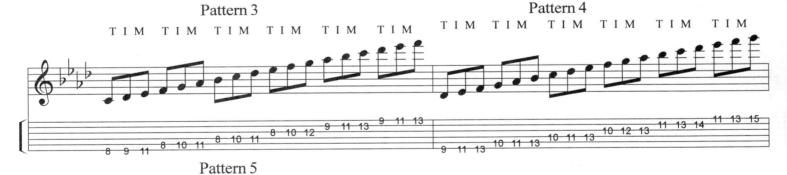

Pattern 5

A MAJOR

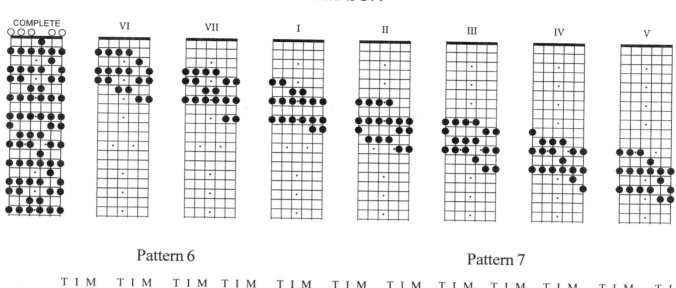

Pattern 6

Pattern 7

Pattern 1

Pattern 2

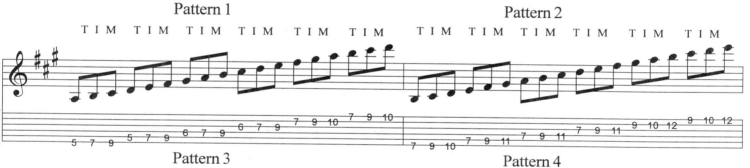

Pattern 3

Pattern 4

Pattern 5

B♭ MAJOR

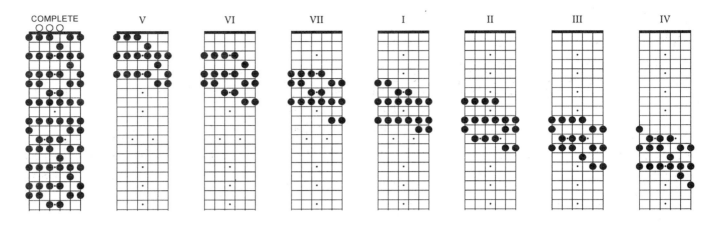

Pattern 5

Pattern 6

Pattern 7

Pattern 1

Pattern 2

Pattern 3

Pattern 4

106

B MAJOR

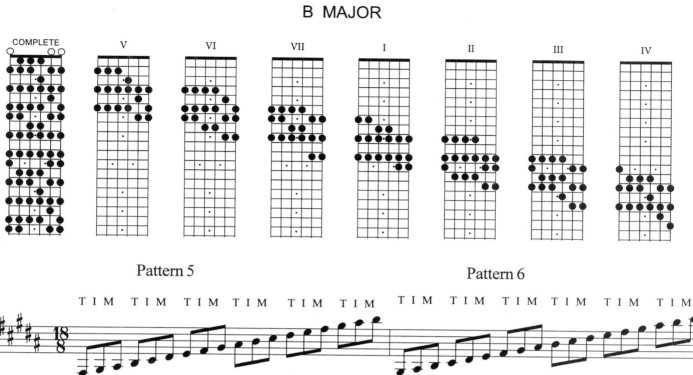

Pattern 5

Pattern 6

Pattern 7

Pattern 1

Pattern 2

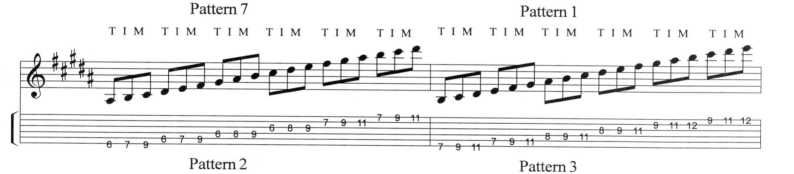

Pattern 3

Pattern 4

C♭ MAJOR

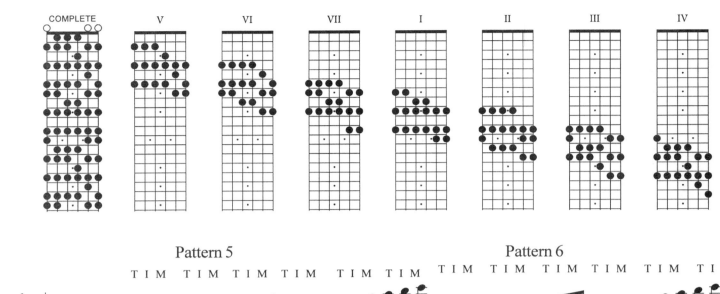

Pattern 5   Pattern 6

Pattern 7   Pattern 1

Pattern 2   Pattern 3

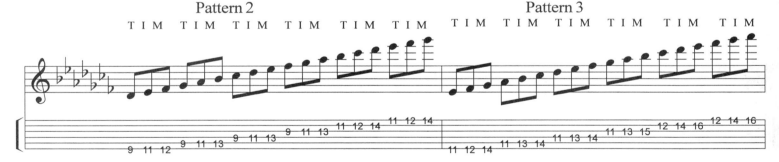

Pattern 4

C♭ Major is the same as B Major. It is included here for the sake of studying the notation.

C MAJOR

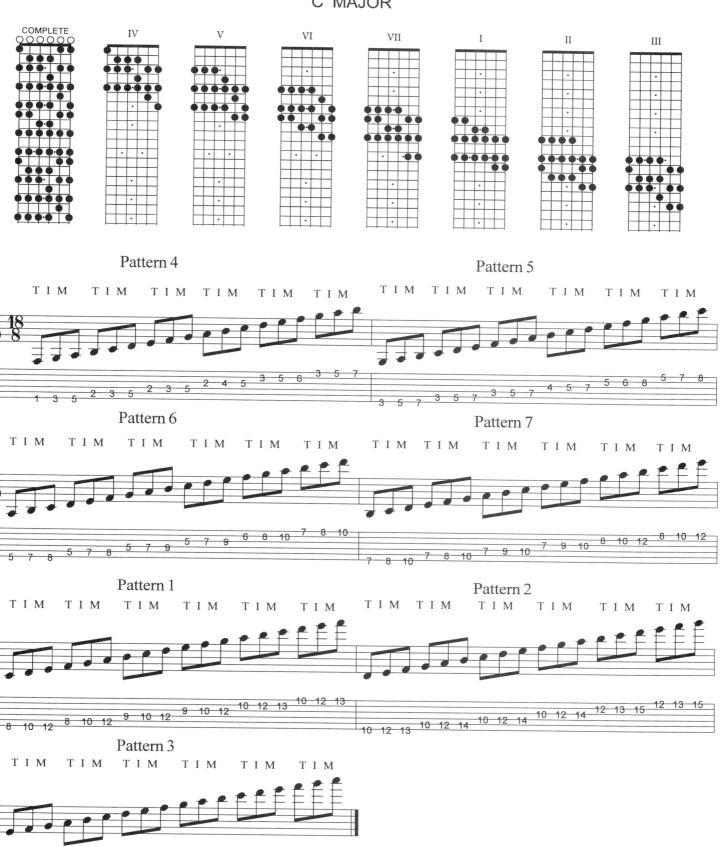

C# MAJOR

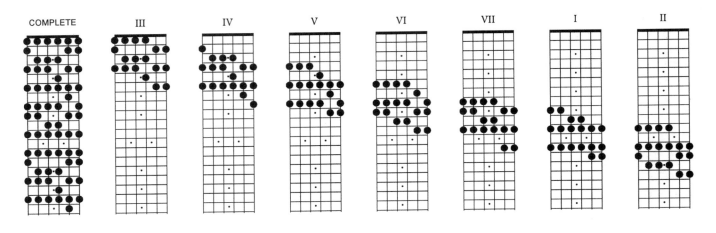

Pattern 3

Pattern 4

Pattern 5

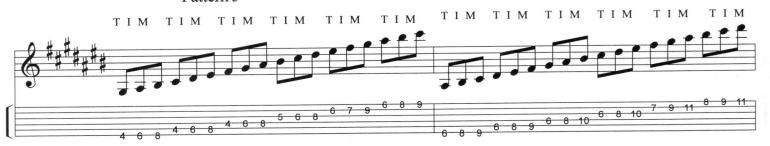

Pattern 6

Pattern 7

Pattern 1

Pattern 2

D♭ MAJOR

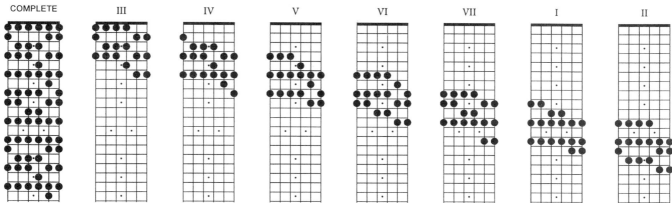

Pattern 3
T I M T I M T I M T I M T I M T I M

Pattern 4
T I M T I M T I M T I M T I M T I M

Pattern 5
T I M T I M T I M T I M T I M T I M

Pattern 6
T I M T I M T I M T I M T I M T I M

Pattern 7
T I M T I M T I M T I M T I M T I M

Pattern 1
T I M T I M T I M T I M T I M T I M

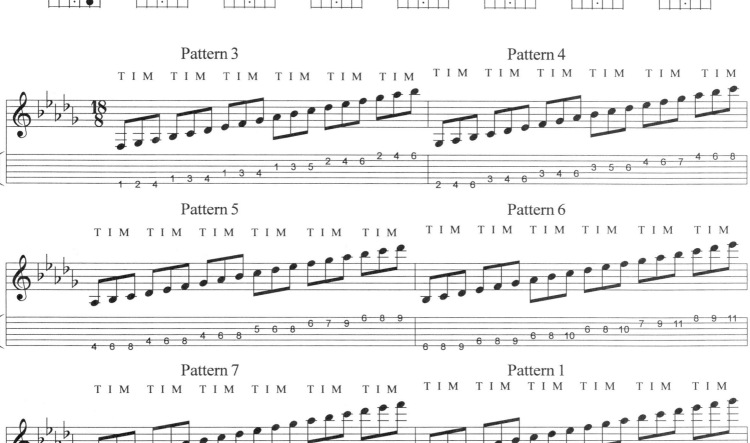

Pattern 2
T I M T I M T I M T I M T I M T I M

D♭ Major is the same as C♯ Major. It is included here for the sake of studying the notation.

D MAJOR

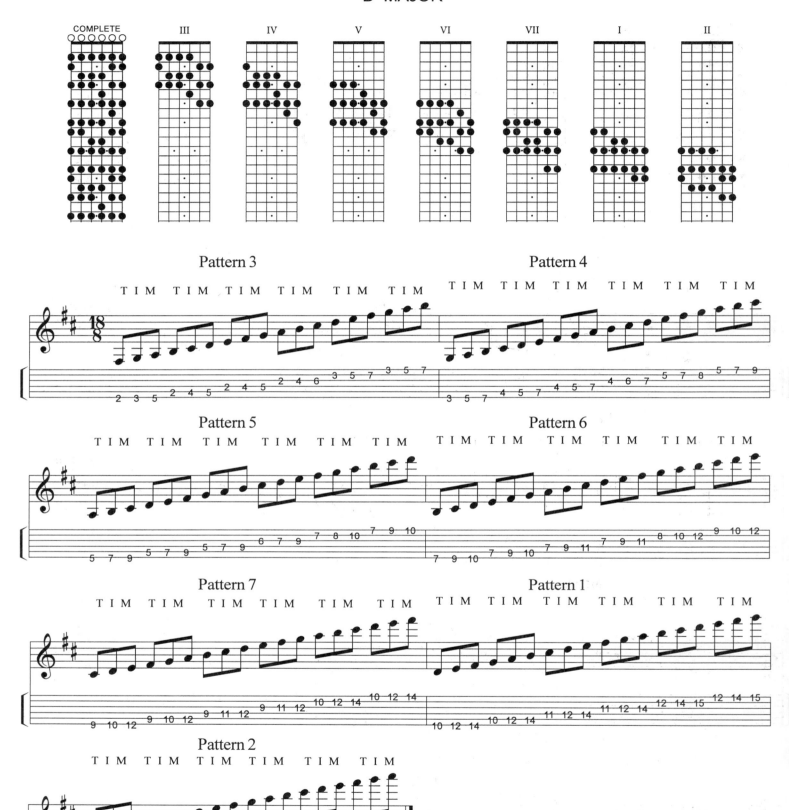

E♭ MAJOR

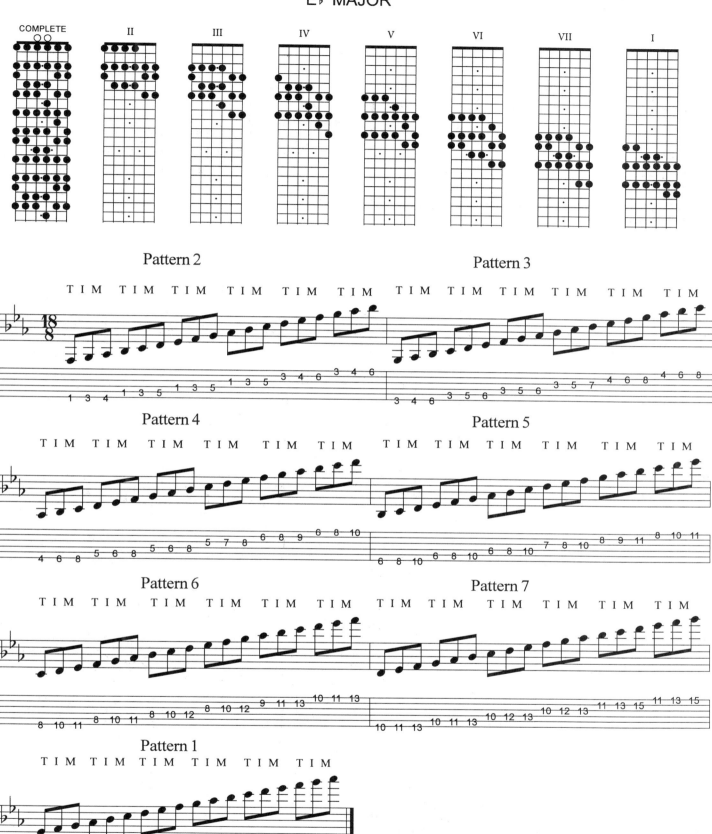

E MAJOR

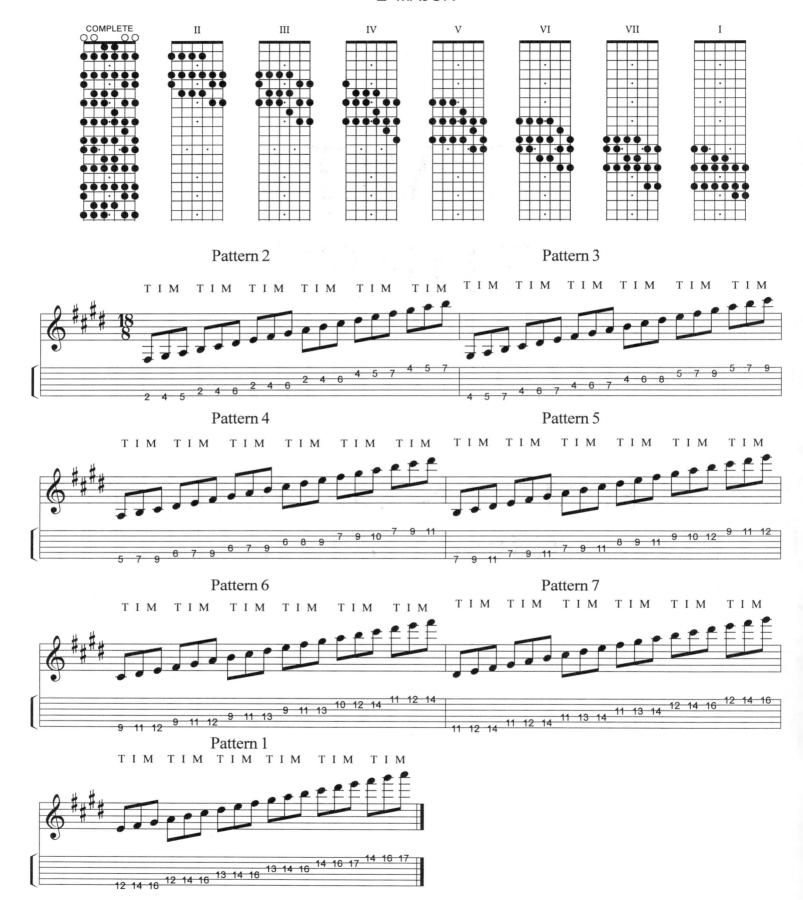

PART THREE

SCALE FINGERPICKING
(Minor Pentatonic)

PRACTICING THE PENTATONICS

Next we learn how to practice the pentatonics. Most of the ground work as to how to practice these scales has been done when you learned the Major scales.

Just like the Major scale breakdown we do the same thing for the Minor Pentatonic. In figure 6 below, the fretboard on the left shows every note possible for the F Minor Pentatonic. The fretboards to the right of it break it down into patterns at various positions.

Below that the patterns are expanded to show what left hand fingerings are used to play the patterns.

F MINOR PENTATONIC

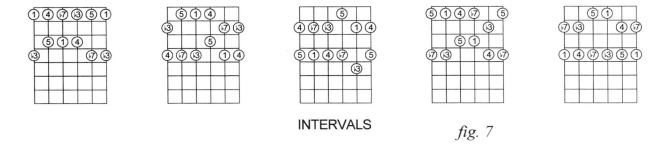

FINGERING

fig. 6

In figure 7 below are the intervals of the patterns of the pentatonic. Just as with the patterns of the Major scale, the intervallic relationship always remains constant even when the notes change after changing keys.

INTERVALS

fig. 7

The notes for the Pentatonic patterns in F Minor are as follows:

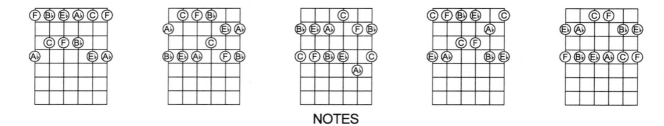

NOTES

The fingerpicking for the Pentatonic Patterns is quite easy. For the ascending from lowest to highest note of the pattern it is T,I,T,I,T,I etc. That is it. The same holds true for all five patterns. You can reverse the pattern to I,T,I,T. This will add a new level to your dexterity. You can also replace the T,I with I,M.

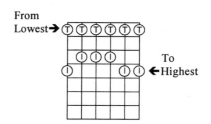

From Lowest → To Highest

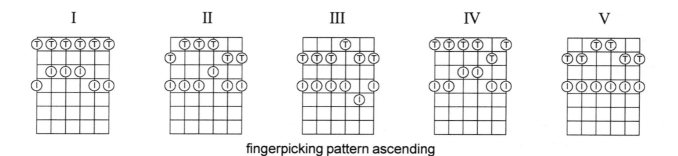

| I | II | III | IV | V |

fingerpicking pattern ascending

F MINOR PENTATONIC (ascending)

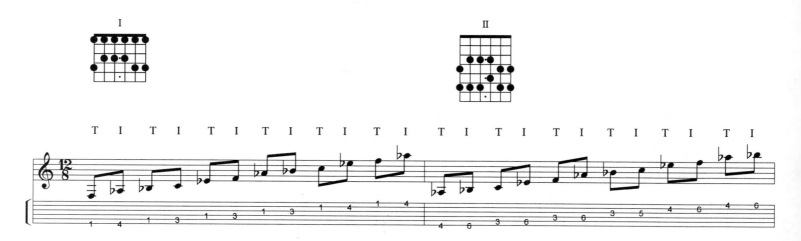

118

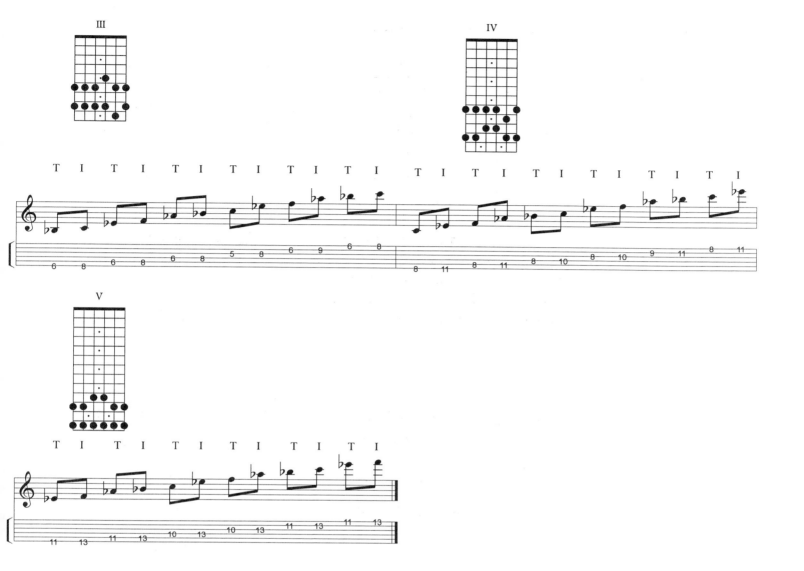

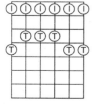 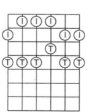 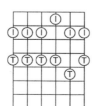 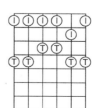 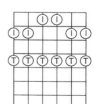

The picking pattern for descending the pentatonic is also T,I,T,I. And you can reverse it to I,T,I,T for dexterity practice.

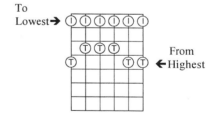

fingerpicking pattern descending

119

F MINOR PENTATONIC (descending)

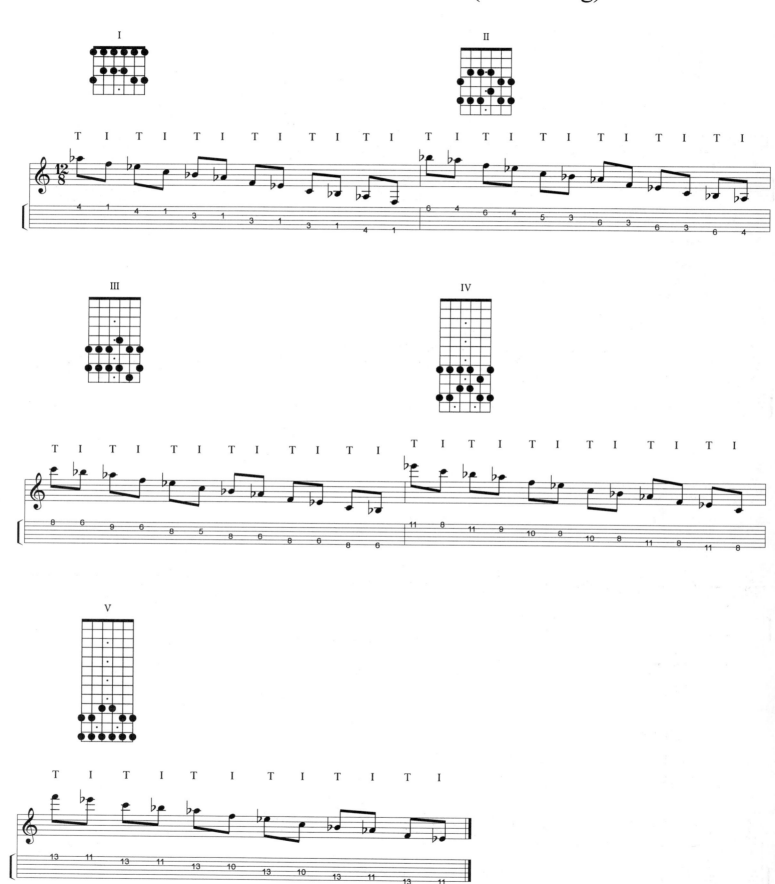

120

F MINOR PENTATONIC (ascending & descending)

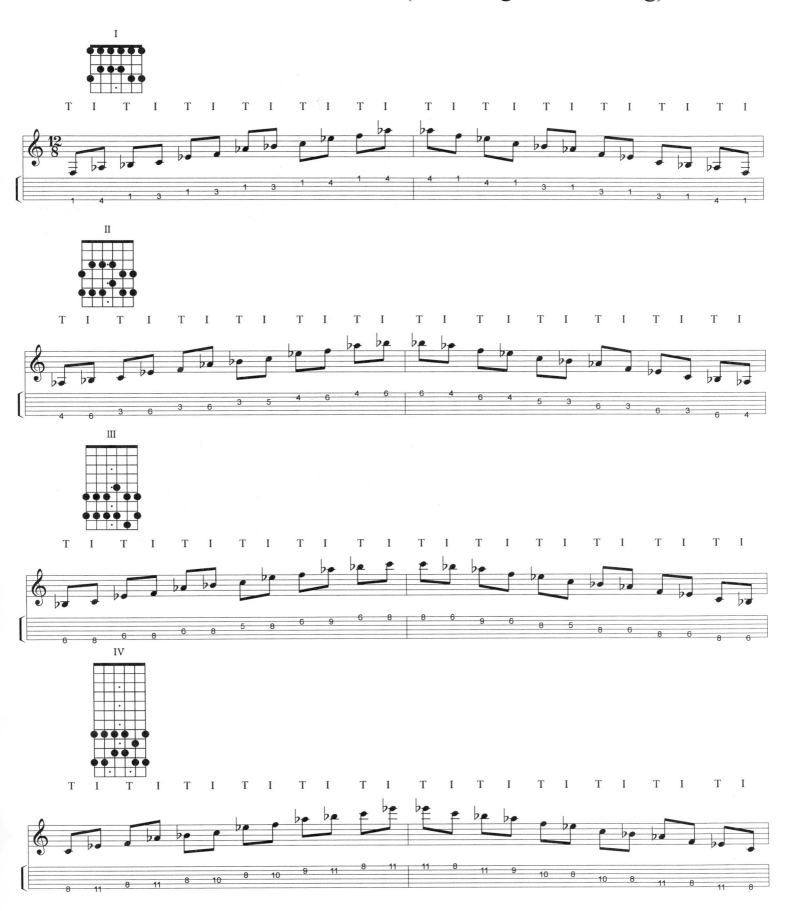

121

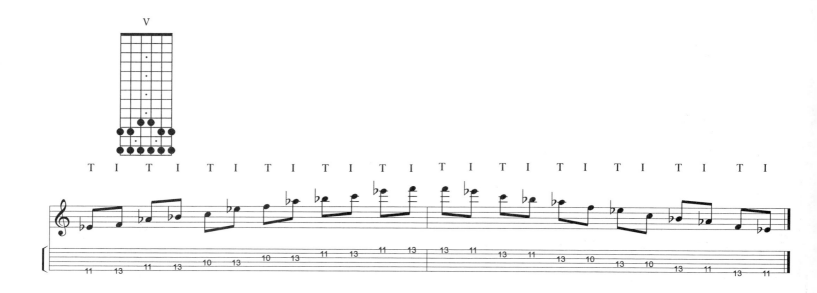

Now we ascend and descend while alternating the patterns.

F MINOR PENTATONIC
(ascending & descending - alternating patterns)

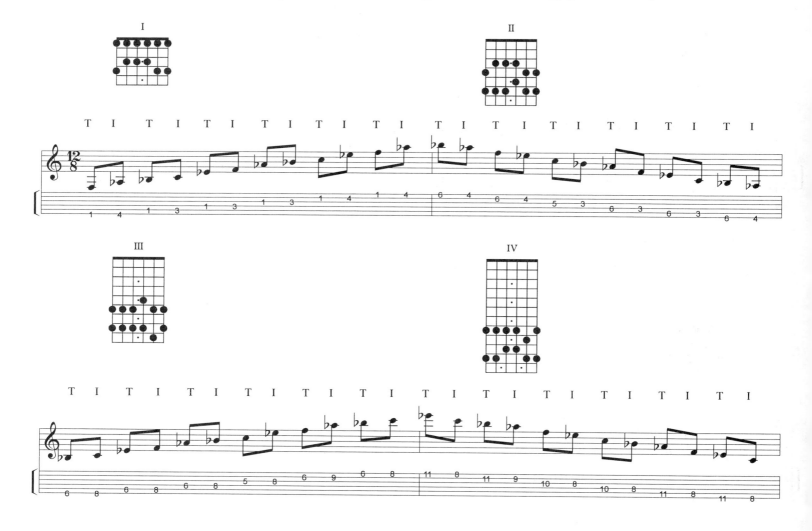

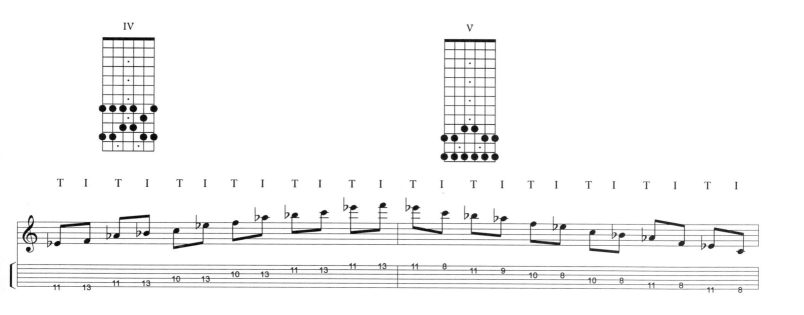

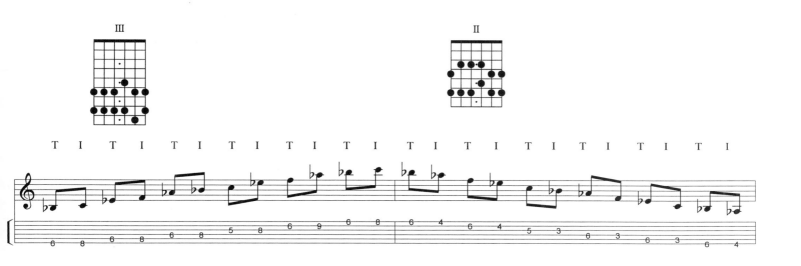

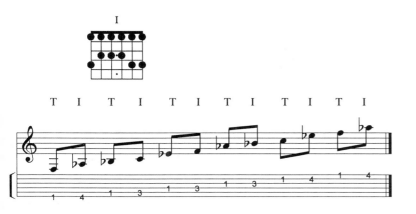

THREE NOTE COIL ASCENDING PICKING PATTERNS
(for pentatonic)

By now we should be familiar with the format used to present these exercises. Just go with the flow of the continuity. The picking is broken up for you using these two pattern groups. Each group represents the fingerpicking action taking place in a measure. Once learned the same fingerpicking patterns applies to all of the pentatonic patterns. Remember, the fingerpicking can also be reversed. Not to mention that you can play it as I,M,I,M,I,M etc. or M,I,M,I,M,I.

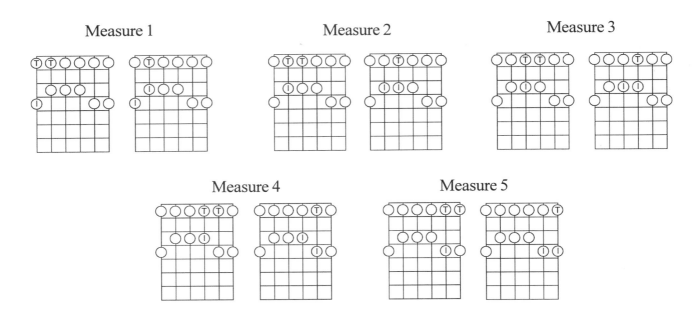

THREE NOTE COILS IN F MINOR PENTATONIC (ascending)

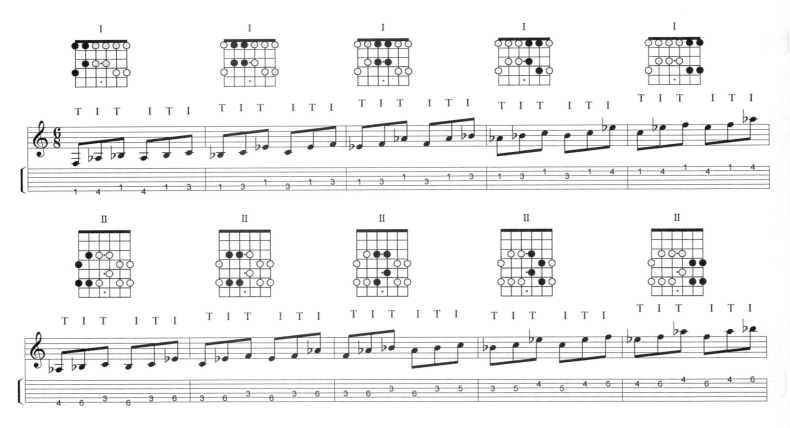

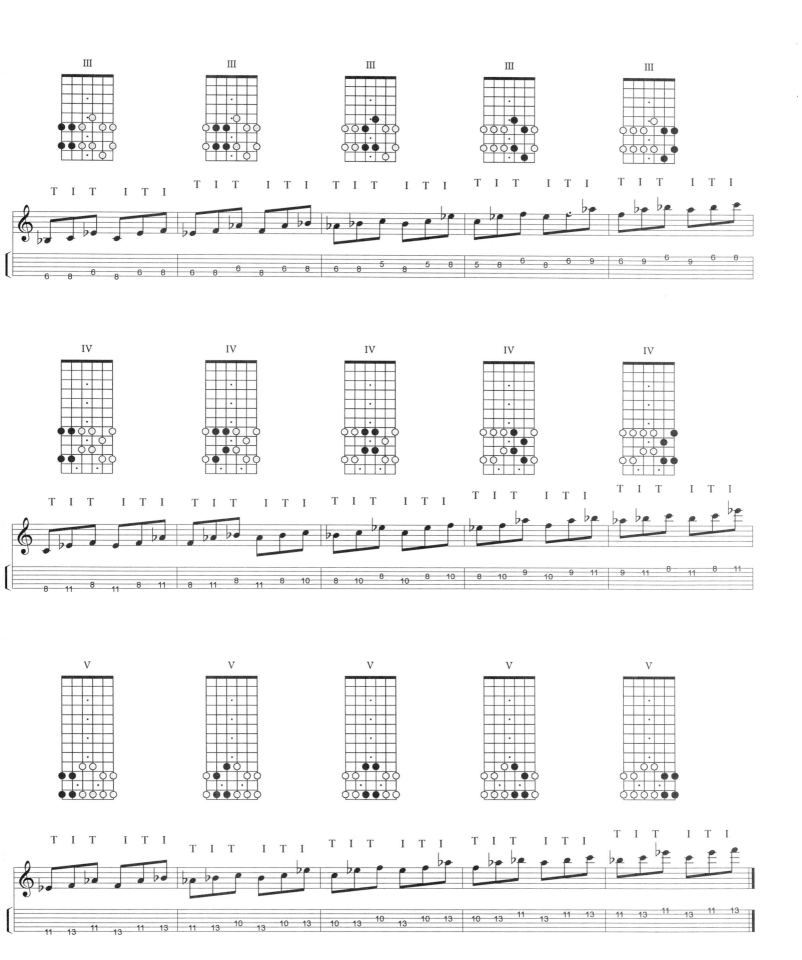

THREE NOTE COIL DESCENDING PICKING PATTERNS
(for pentatonic)

OK! Now we learn to descend the pentatonic three note coils. Learn the fingerpicking pattern and go to it.

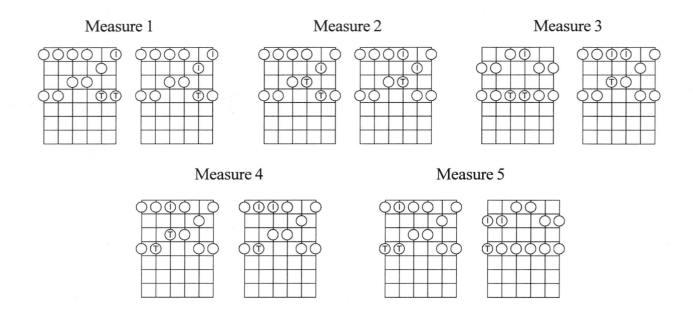

THREE NOTE COILS IN F MINOR PENTATONIC (descending)

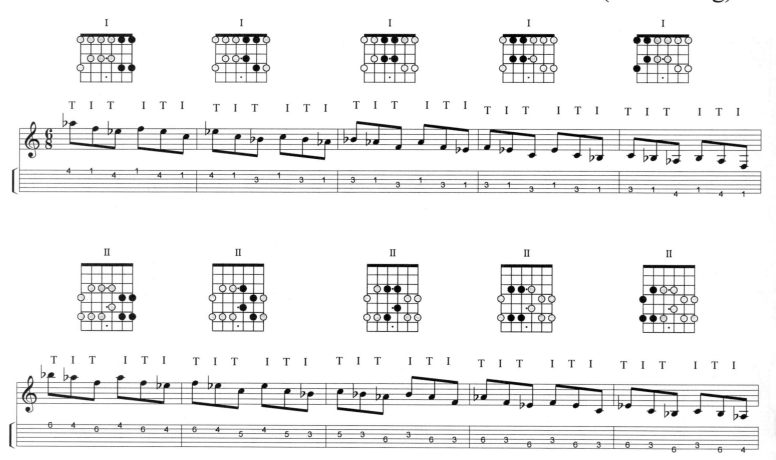

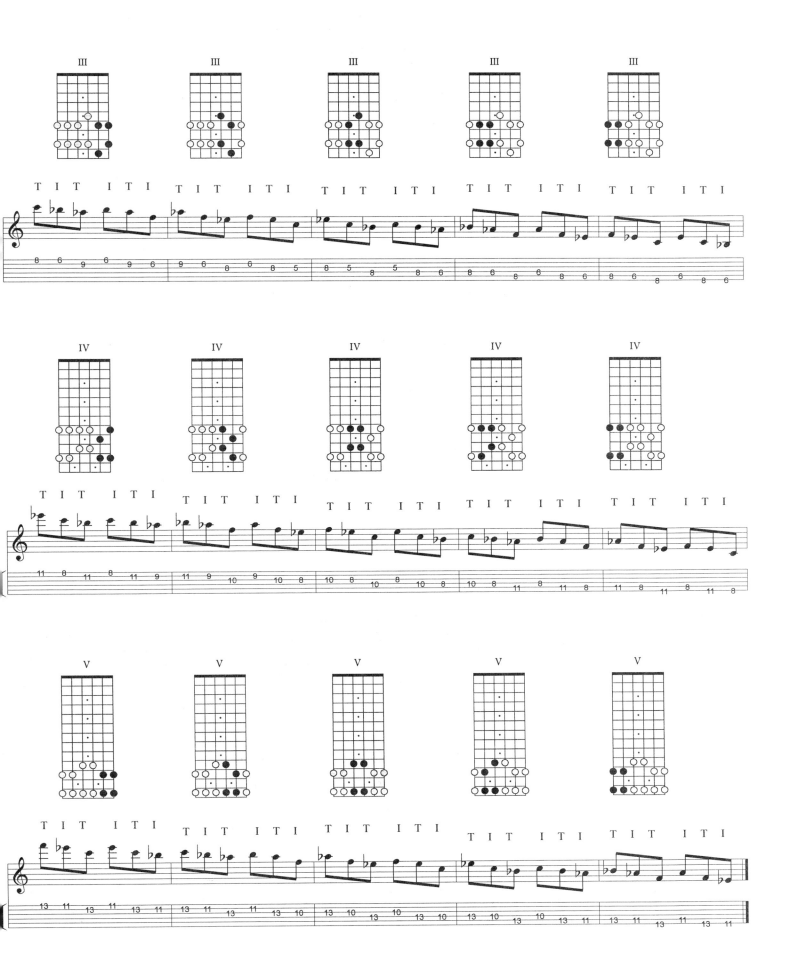

127

THREE NOTE COILS IN F MINOR PENTATONIC
(ascending & descending)

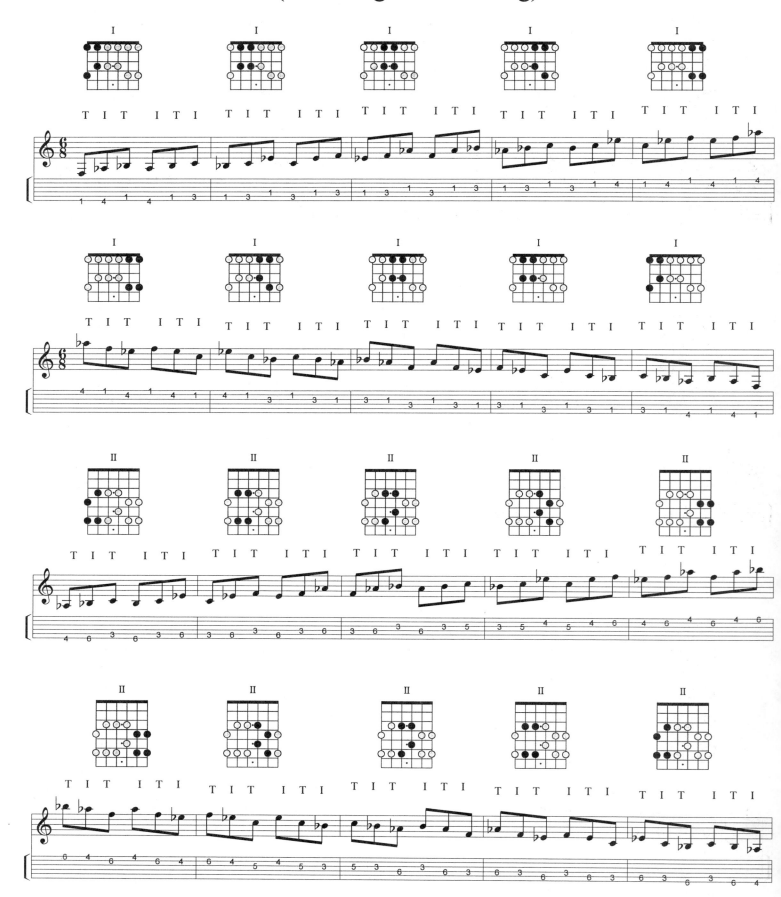

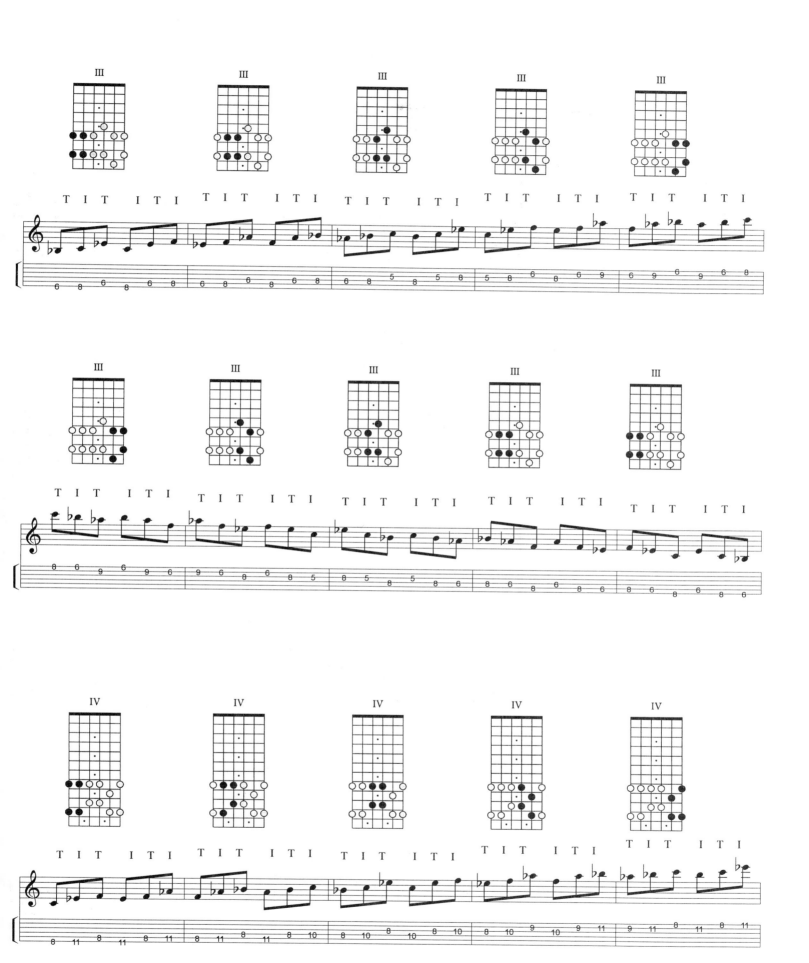

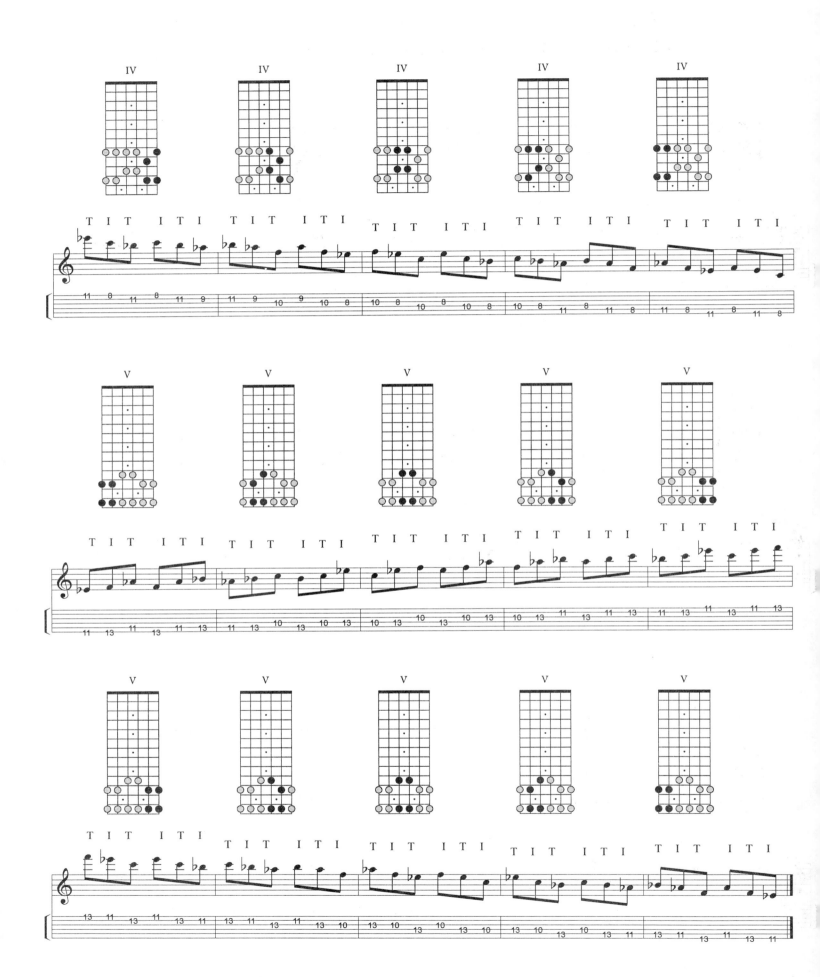

130

THREE NOTE COILS IN F MINOR PENTATONIC
(ascending & descending - alternating patterns)

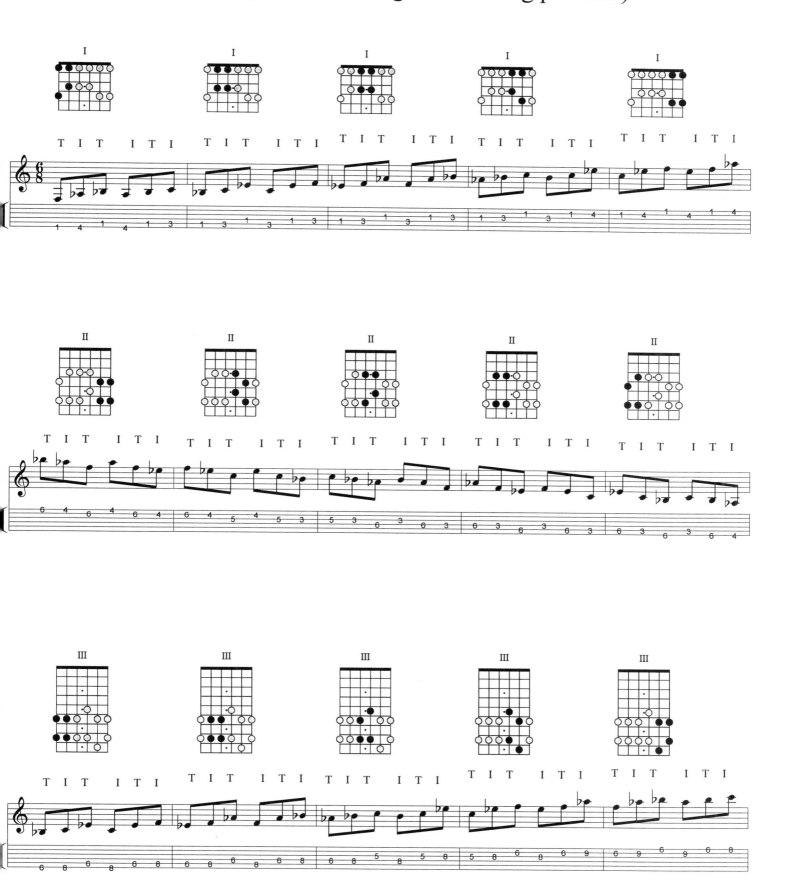

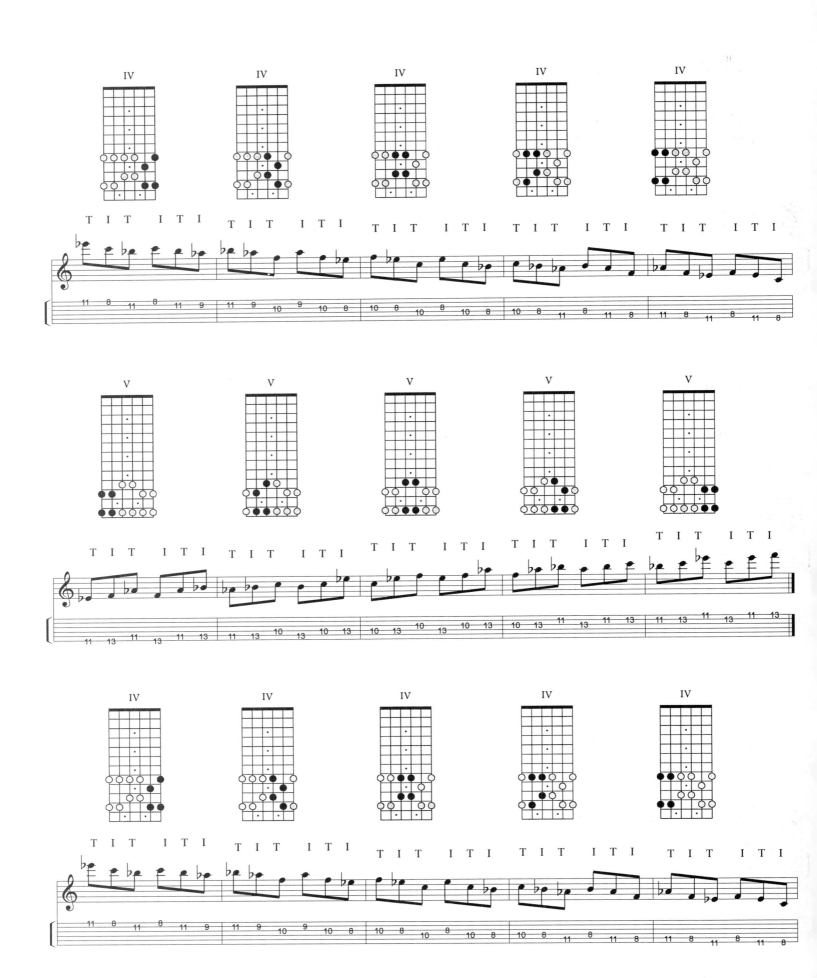

132

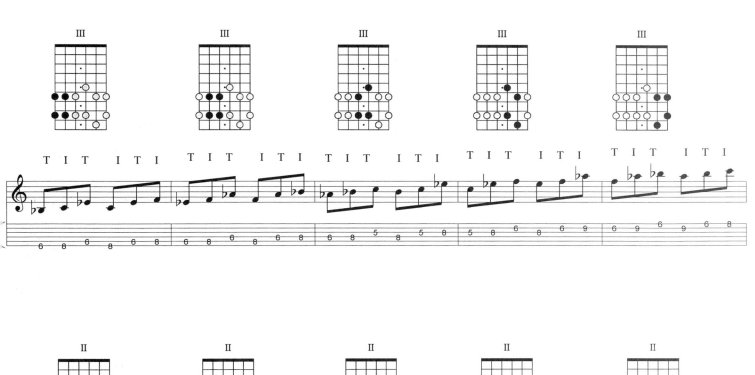

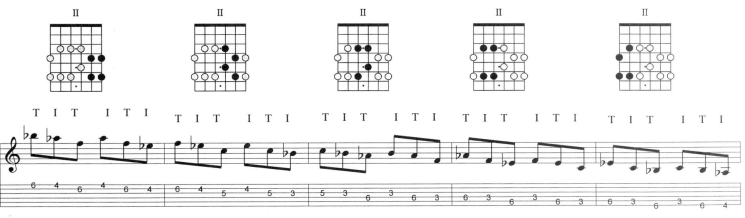

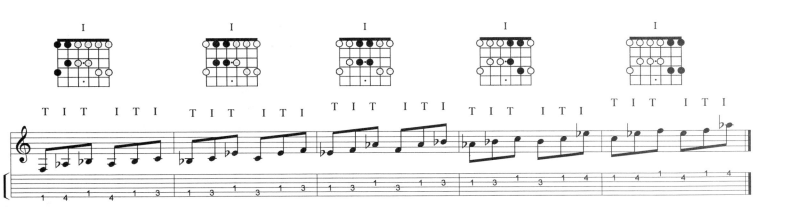

FOUR NOTE COIL ASCENDING PICKING PATTERNS
(for pentatonic)

Now we do the four note coils for the Minor pentatonic. Here are the fingerpicking patterns. Now go for it.

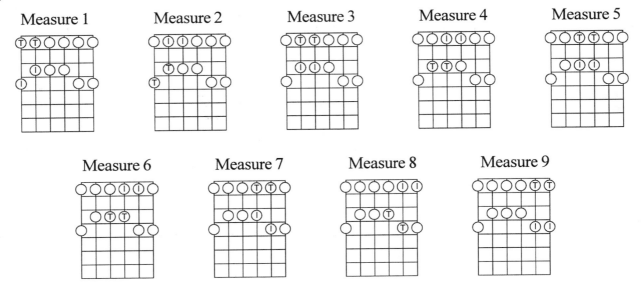

You can also replace the T,I,T,I with T,I,M,R.

FOUR NOTE COILS IN F MINOR PENTATONIC (ascending)

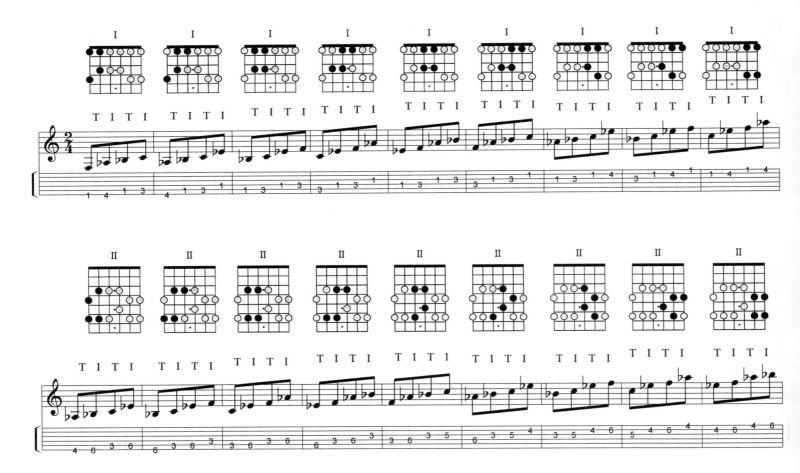

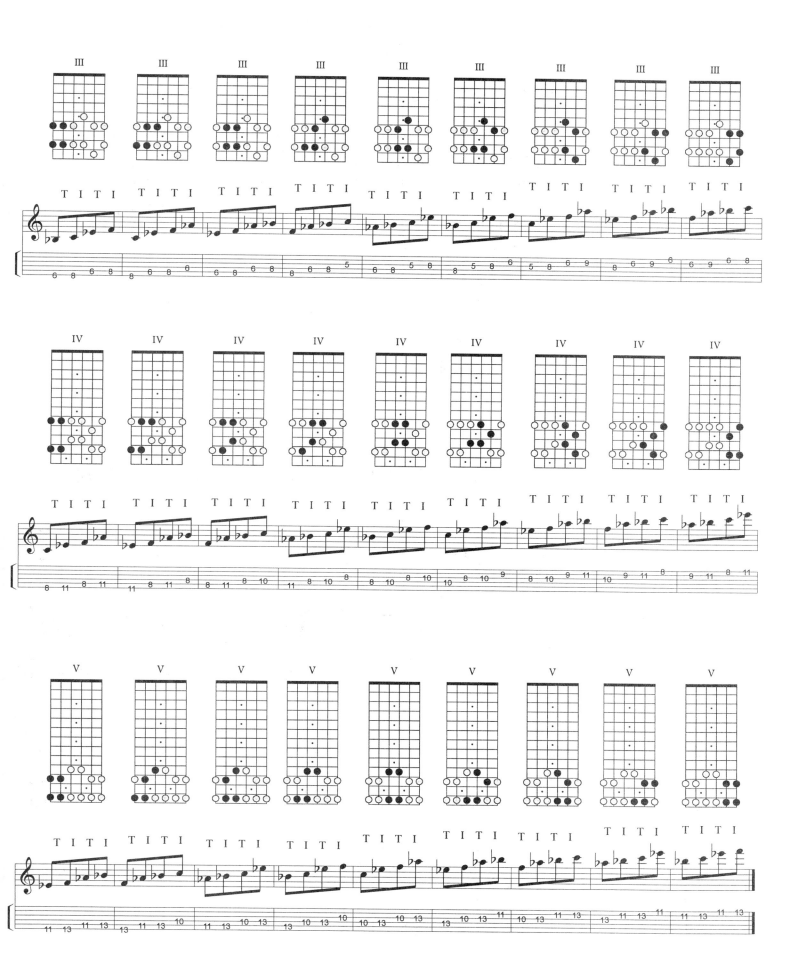

135

FOUR NOTE COIL DESCENDING PICKING PATTERNS
(for pentatonic)

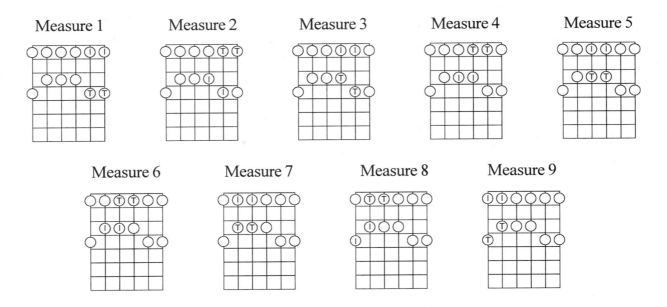

You can replace the T,I,T,I with T,I,M,R.

FOUR NOTE COILS IN F MINOR PENTATONIC (descending)

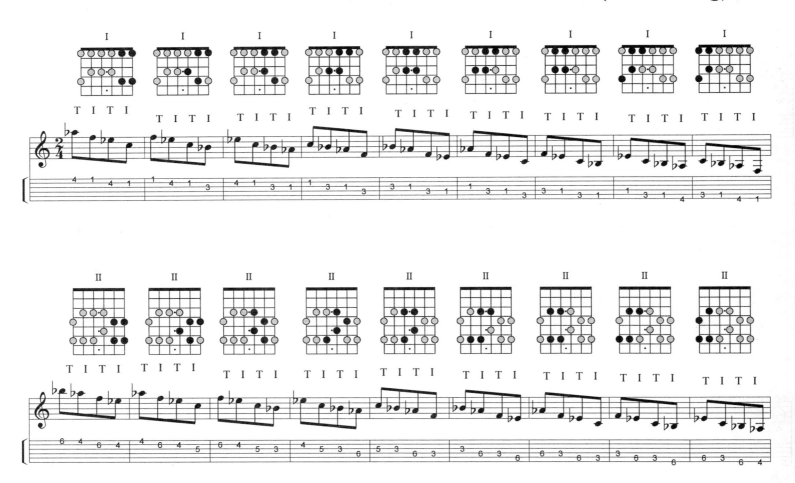

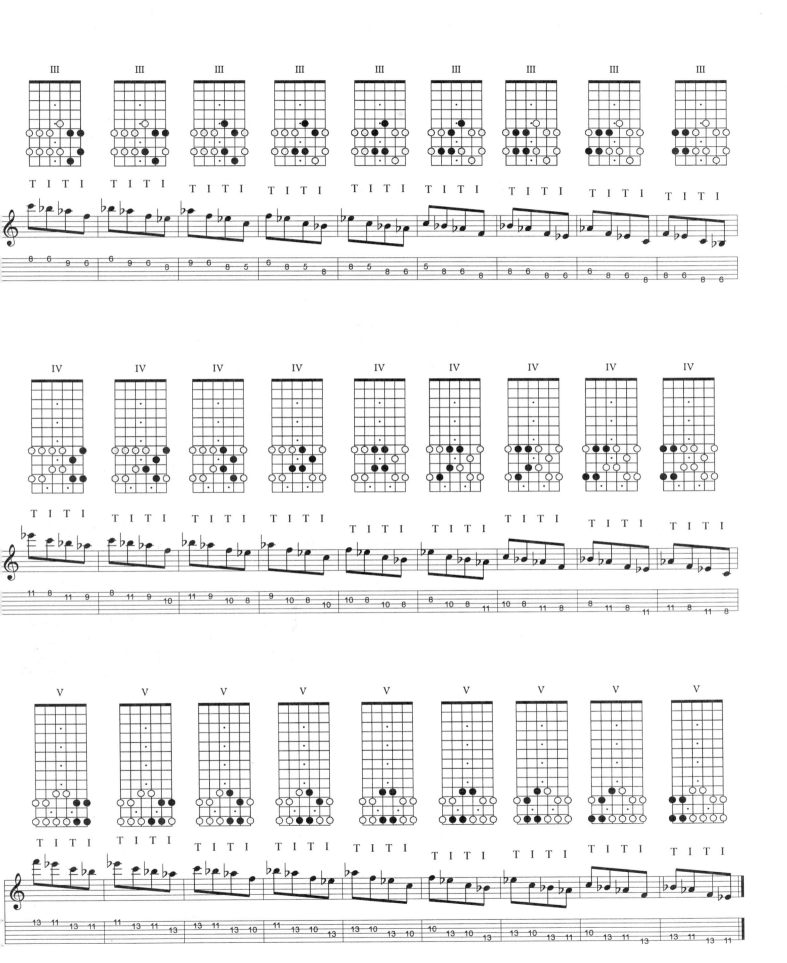

137

FOUR NOTE COILS IN F MINOR PENTATONIC
(ascending & descending)

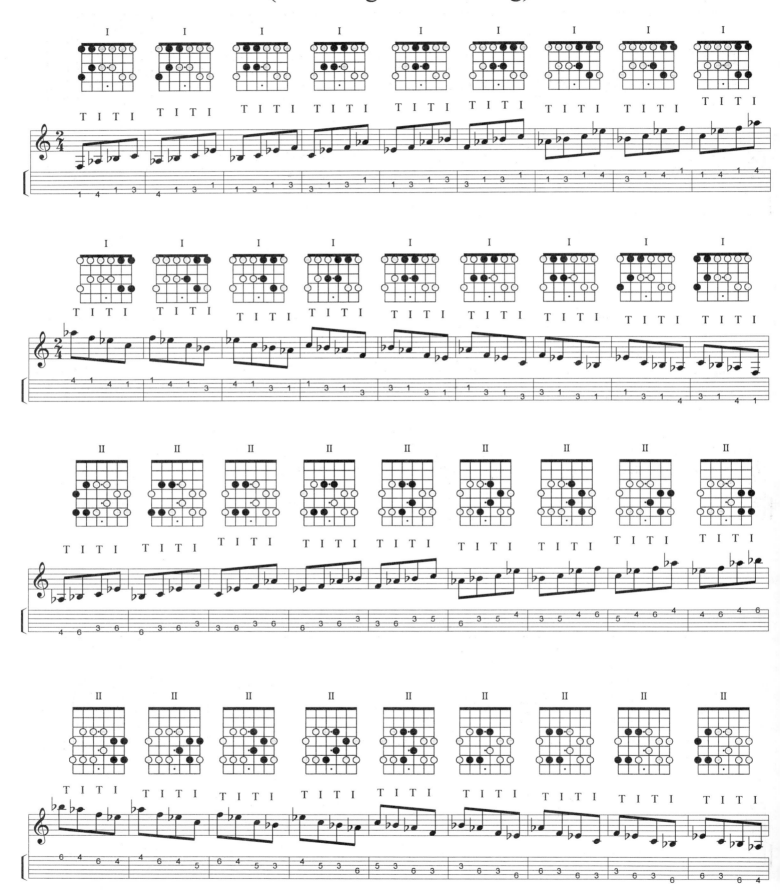

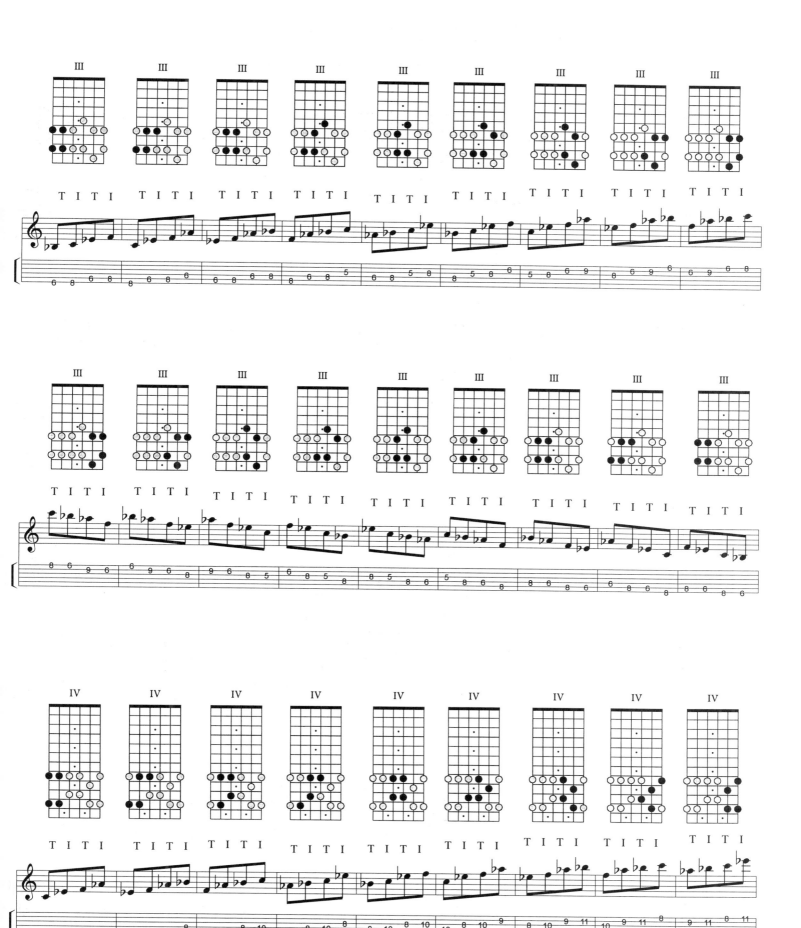

139

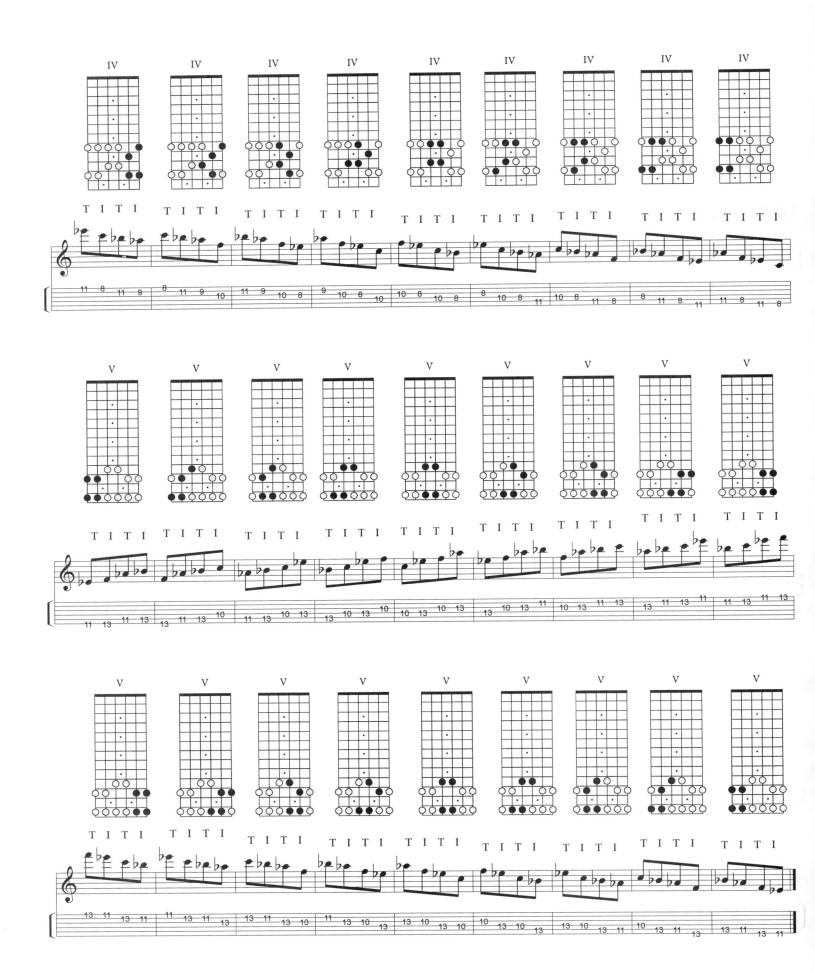

140

FOUR NOTE COILS IN F MINOR PENTATONIC
(ascending & descending - alternating patterns)

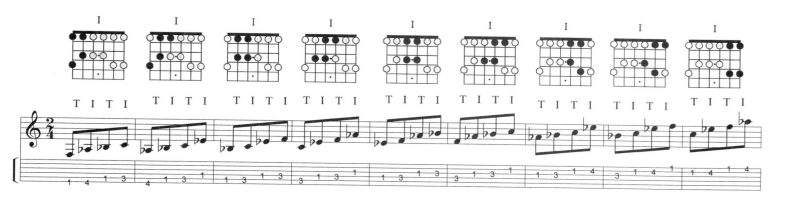

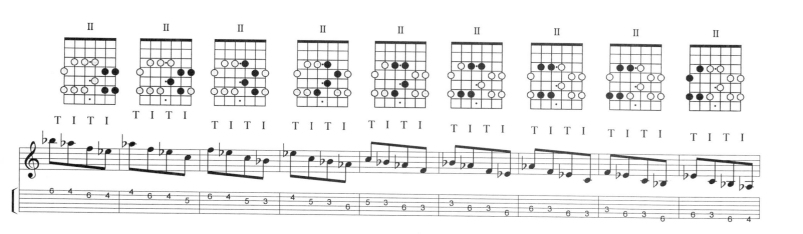

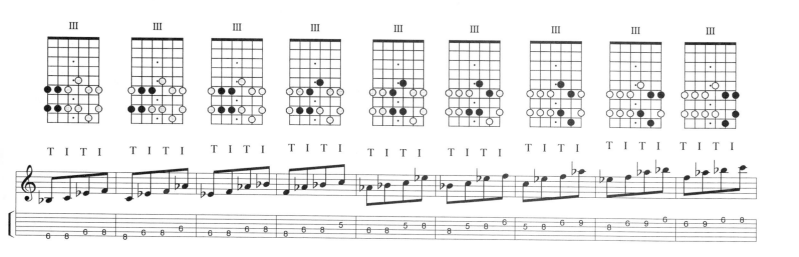

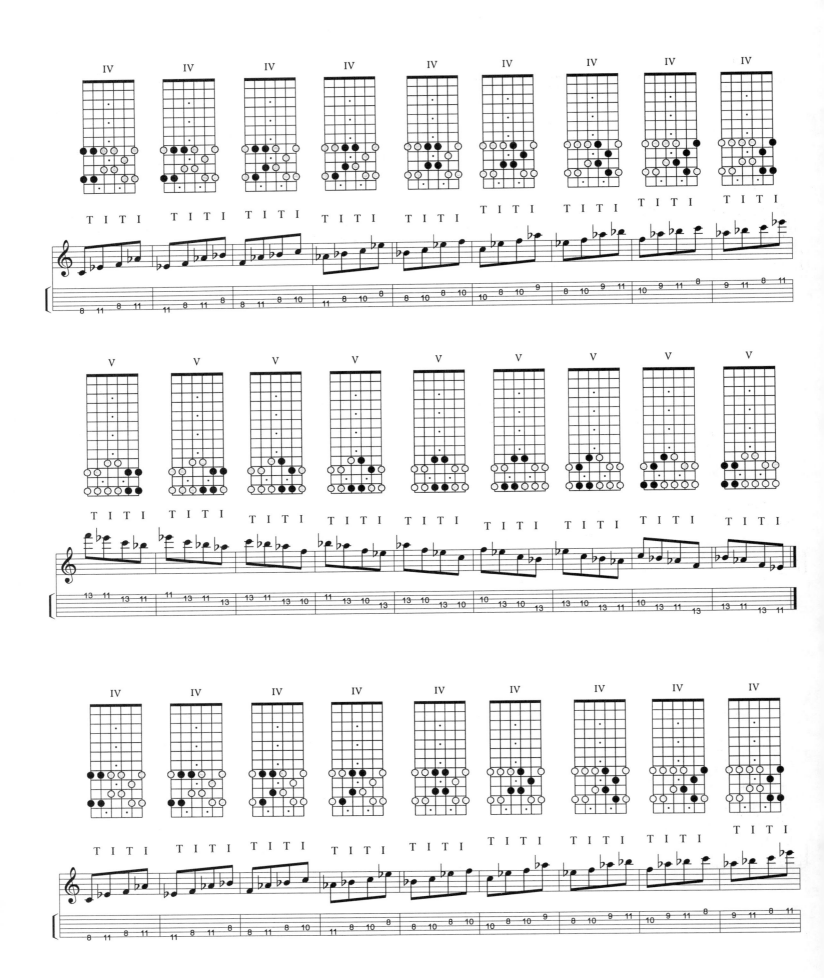

142

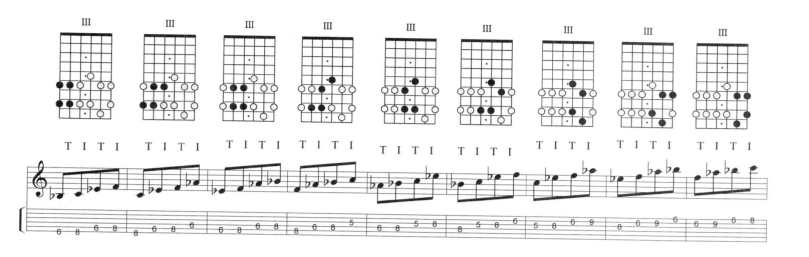

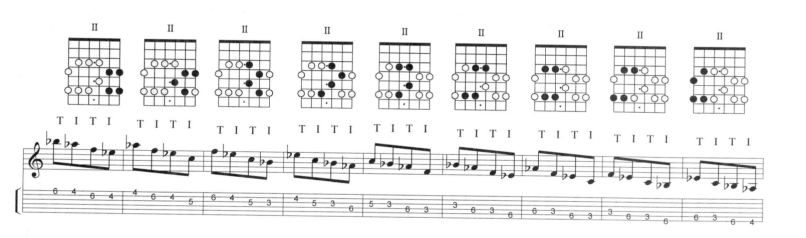

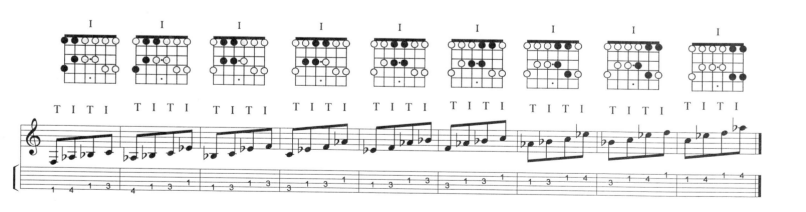

TWO STRING PENTATONIC EXERCISES

These two string exercises are designed to create the dexterity needed to change patterns from any string. The T,I,T,I,T,I can be played as T,I,M,T,I,M.

THREE NOTE EXERCISE

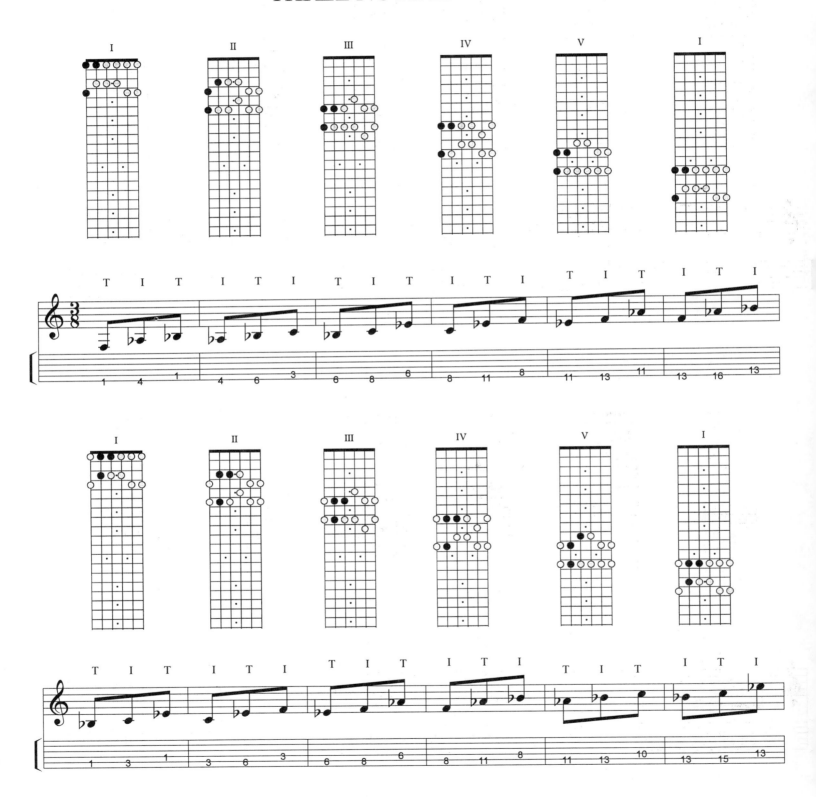

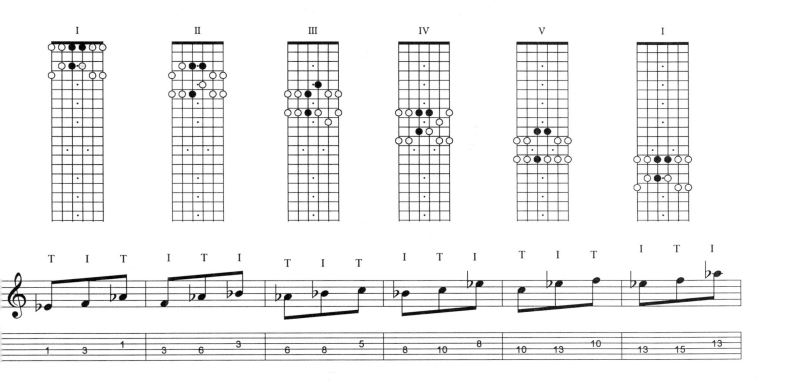

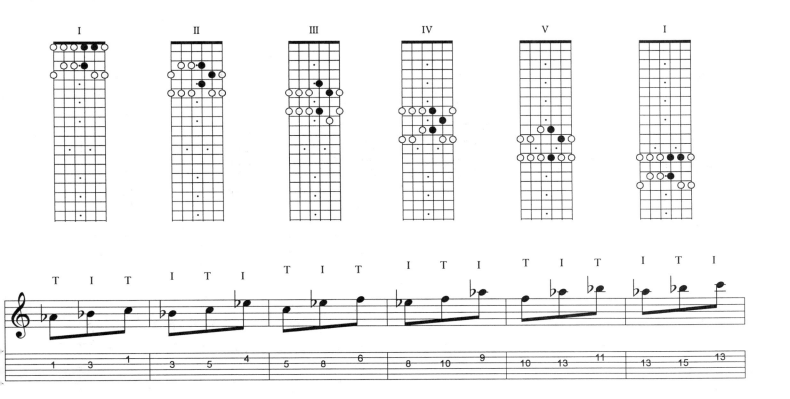

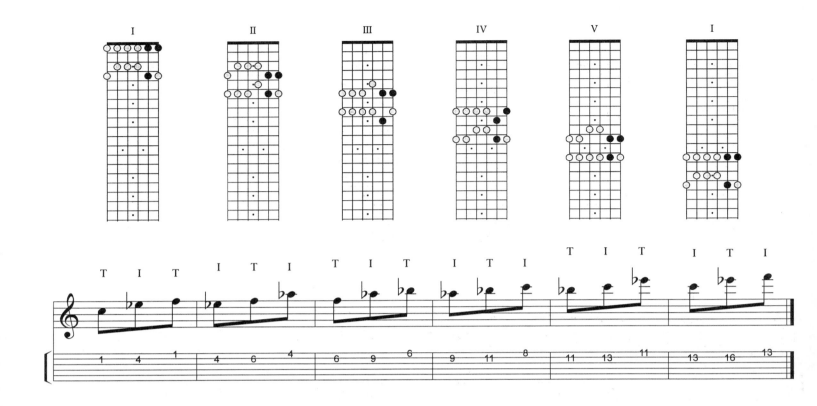

FOUR NOTE EXERCISE

The T,I,T,I can be replaced with T,I,M,R.

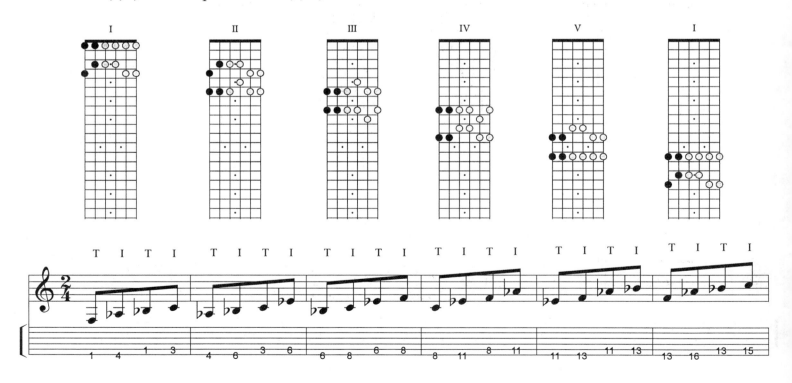

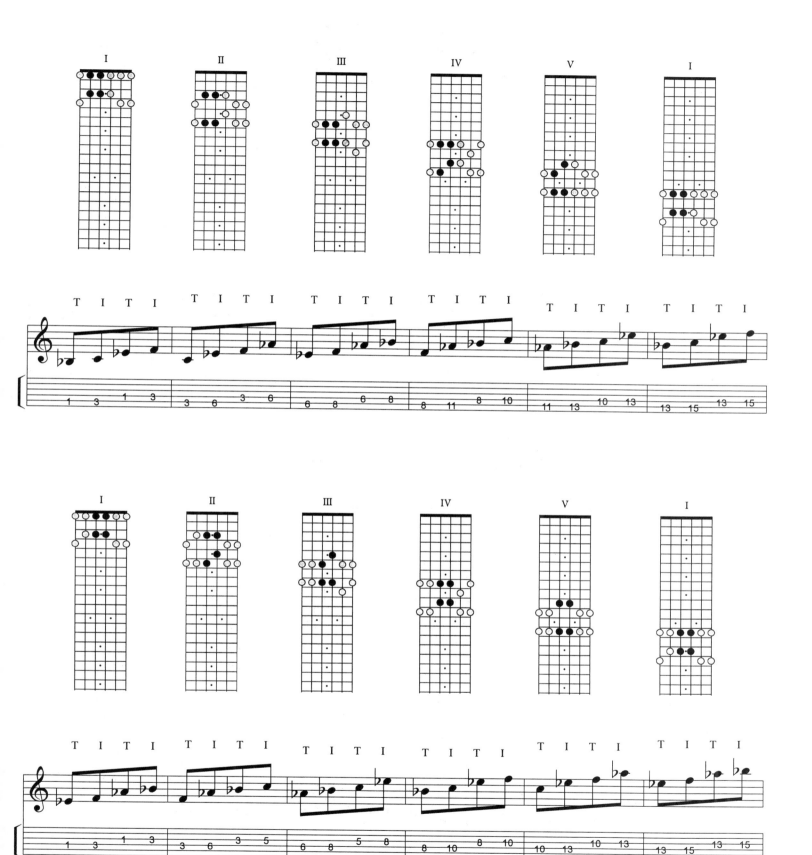

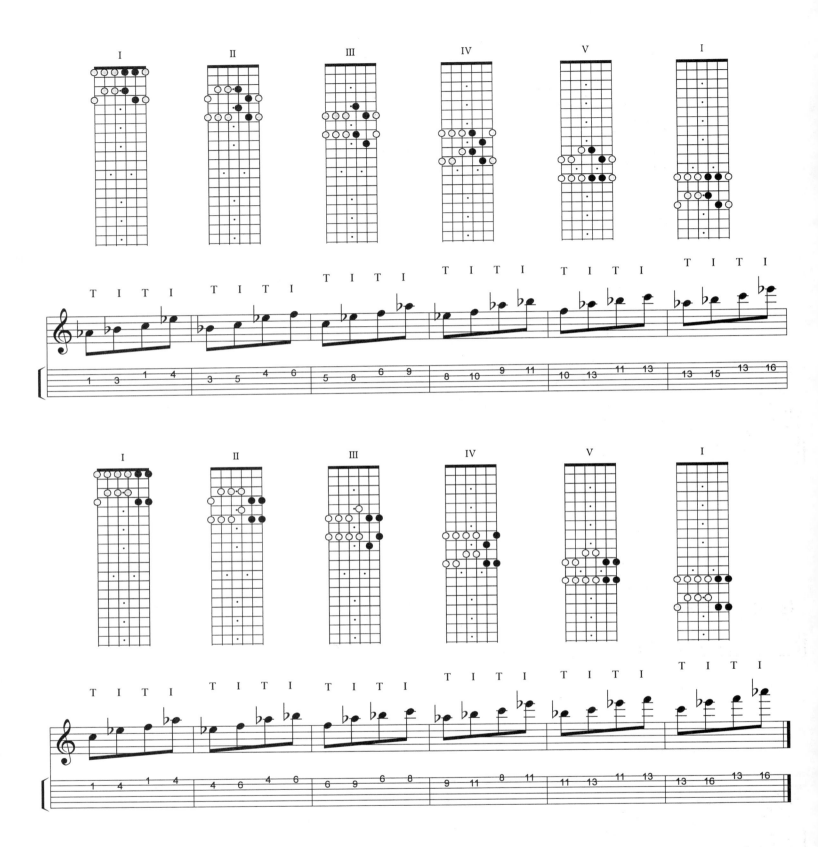

The following pages show the Minor Pentatonic in the other keys. I did not include the enharmonic keys (Gb, Cb, Db, etc.) because there are no key signatures involved. Just as with the Major scale, all the exercises learned for the F Minor Pentatonic can be applied to the other keys. The fingerpicking for the following pages is T, I, T, I.

F♯ MINOR PENTATONIC

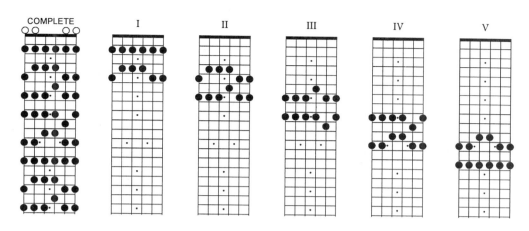

Pattern 1   Pattern 2

Pattern 3   Pattern 4

Pattern 5

G MINOR PENTATONIC

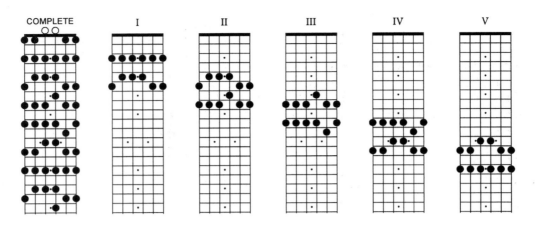

Pattern 1   Pattern 2

Pattern 3   Pattern 4

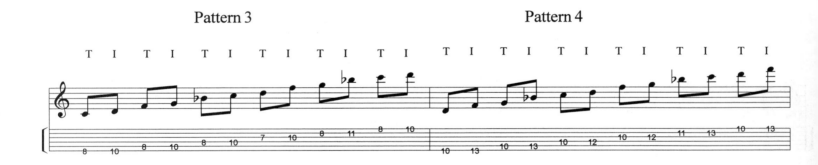

Pattern 5

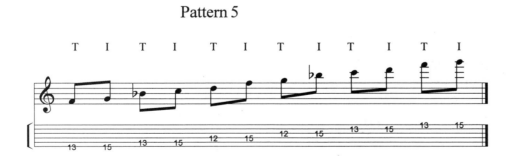

150

A♭ MINOR PENTATONIC

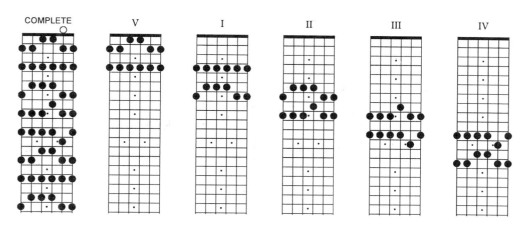

Pattern 5

Pattern 1

Pattern 2

Pattern 3

Pattern 4

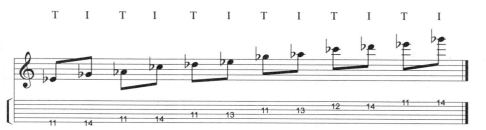

A MINOR PENTATONIC

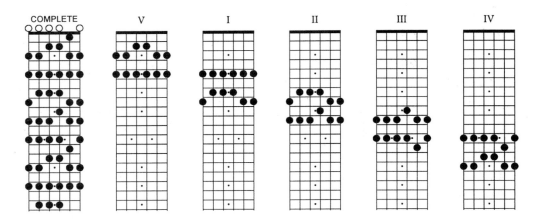

Pattern 5   Pattern 1

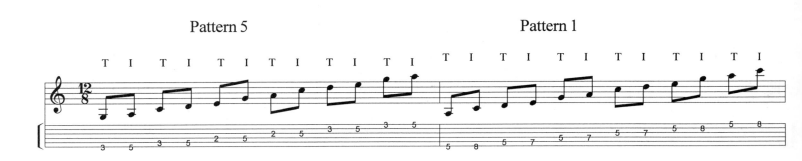

Pattern 2   Pattern 3

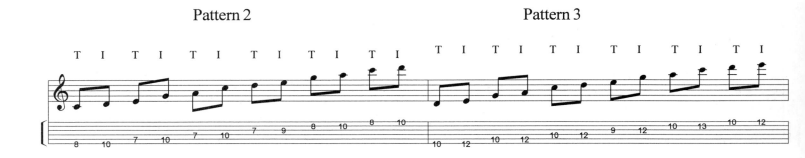

Pattern 4

B♭ MINOR PENTATONIC

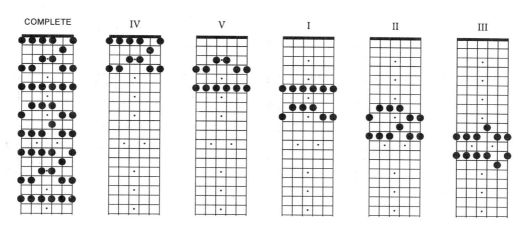

Pattern 4

Pattern 5

Pattern 1

Pattern 2

Pattern 3

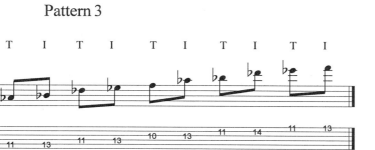

B MINOR PENTATONIC

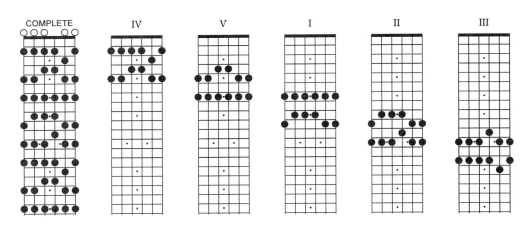

Pattern 4

Pattern 5

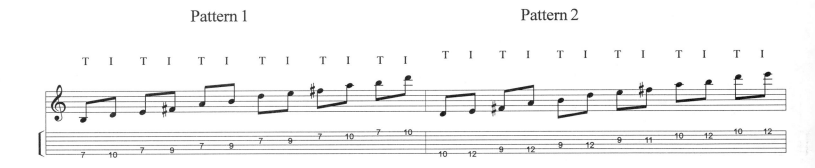

Pattern 1

Pattern 2

Pattern 3

C MINOR PENTATONIC

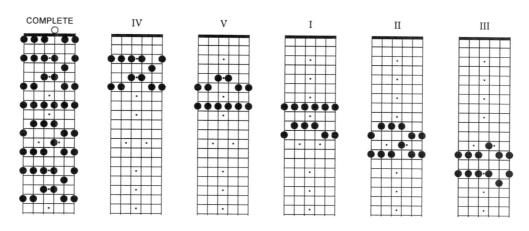

Pattern 4

Pattern 5

Pattern 1
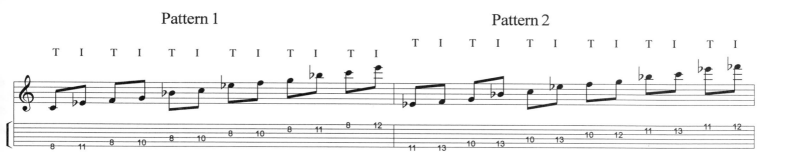

Pattern 2

Pattern 3
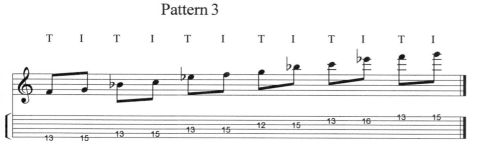

C# MINOR PENTATONIC

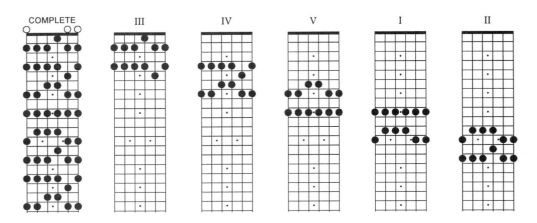

Pattern 3

Pattern 4

Pattern 5

Pattern 1

Pattern 2

D MINOR PENTATONIC

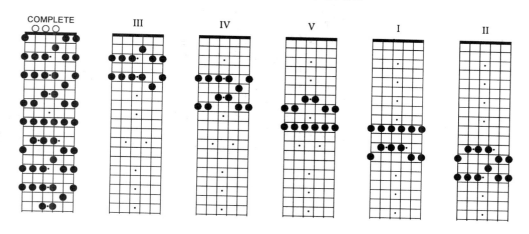

Pattern 3

Pattern 4

Pattern 5

Pattern 1

Pattern 2

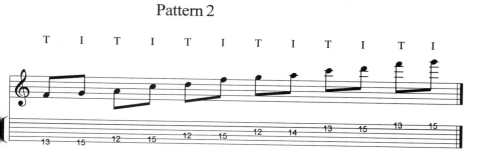

Eb MINOR PENTATONIC

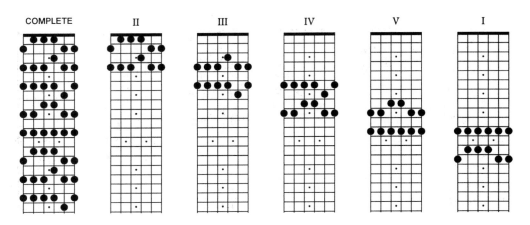

Pattern 2

Pattern 3

Pattern 4

Pattern 5

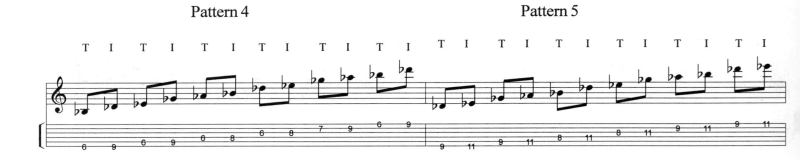

Pattern 1

158

E MINOR PENTATONIC

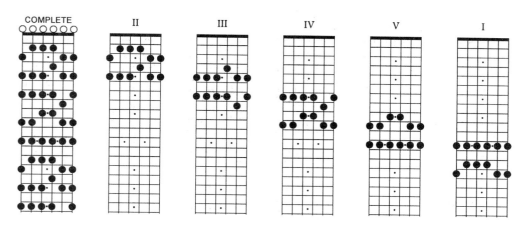

Pattern 2

Pattern 3

Pattern 4

Pattern 5

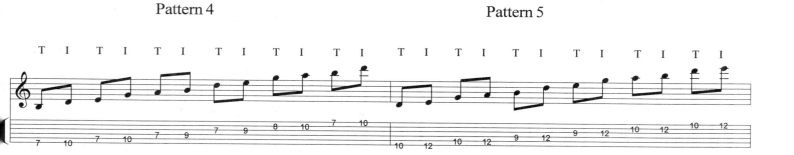

Pattern 1

PART FOUR

OSTINATO BASS

OPEN D OSTINATO BASS

The last important thing to cover regarding fingerpicking is the ostinato bass while doing melodies or chords over it at the same time. This is one of the hardest things to learn. It will take much patience, practice and time. Usually this is taught by transcribing a complete song. The song has to then be broken down by measure anyway in order to learn it. So I presented it in a series of one measure exercises.

First you will tune your low E to a D. Then use the thumb to play the two D's in eighths. When I first started learning this I popped in some of my favorite movies and just played this over and over until the thumb thing was second nature. The low D you will count as 1,2,3,4 and the high D will be the up beats or the &'s. This will set the foundation in helping you to count out the more complex patterns you will be creating down the road.

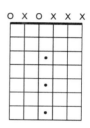
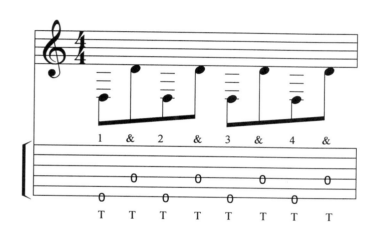

OPEN D OSTINATO BASS WITH THIRD STRING

All of these upcoming examples are just going to use the third string. The notes in the first four examples will strike the note on the first beat.

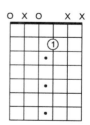
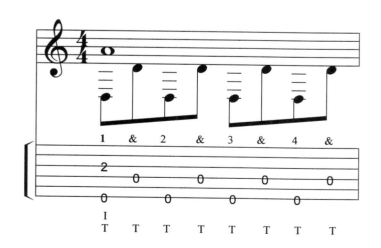

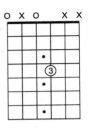

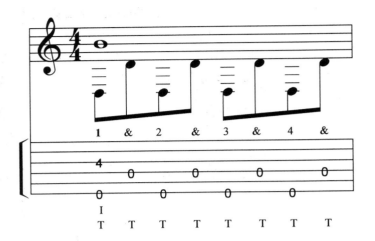

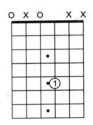

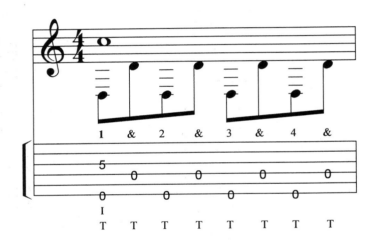

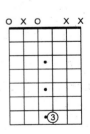

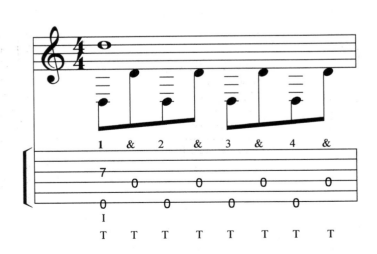

164

All of these examples are on the two beat.

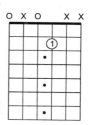

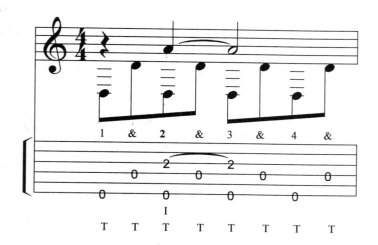

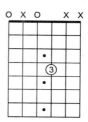

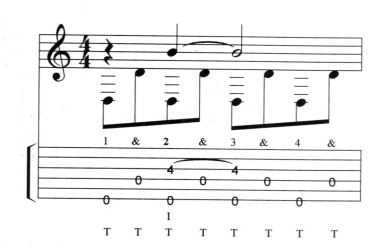

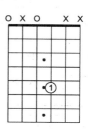

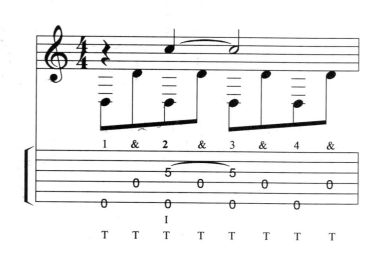

165

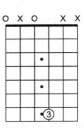

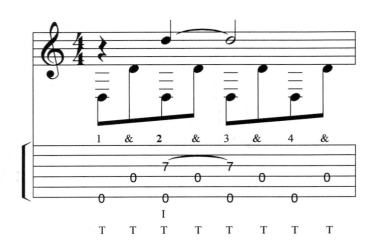

All of these examples are on the three beat.

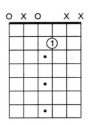

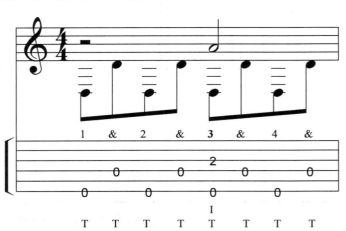

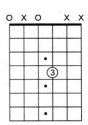

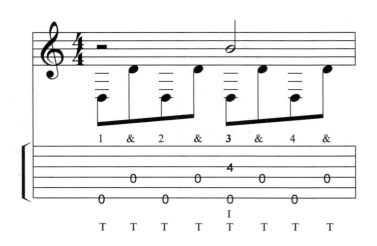

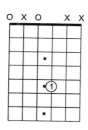

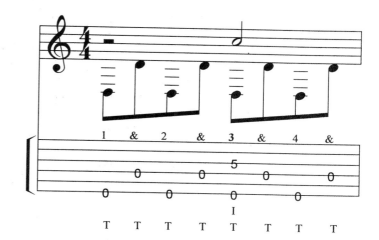

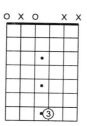

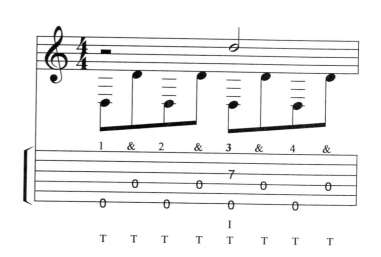

All of these examples are on the four beat.

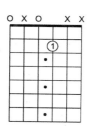

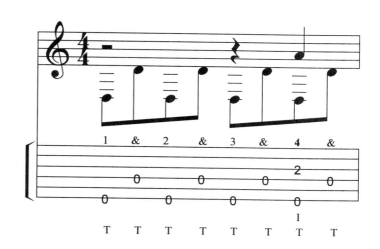

167

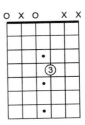

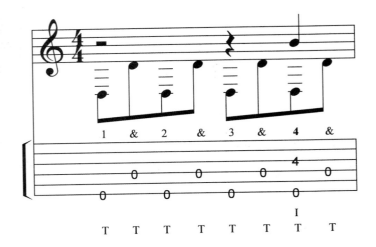

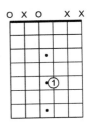

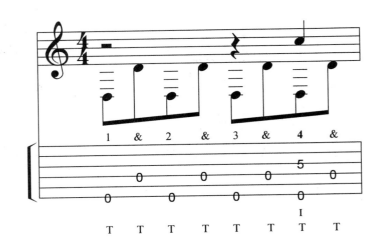

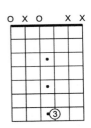

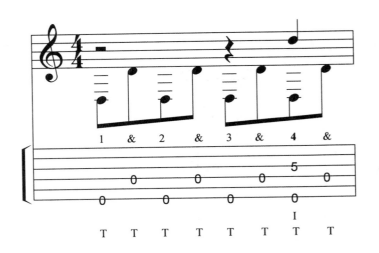

All of these examples are on the one and three beats.

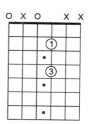

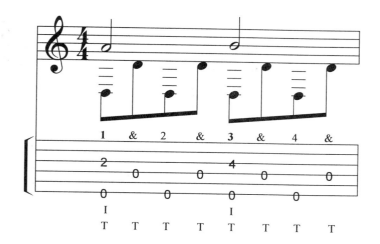

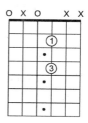

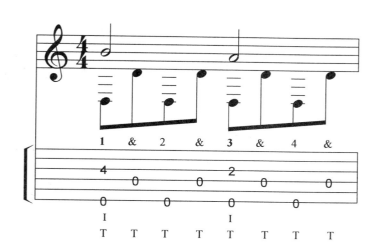

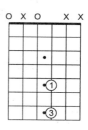

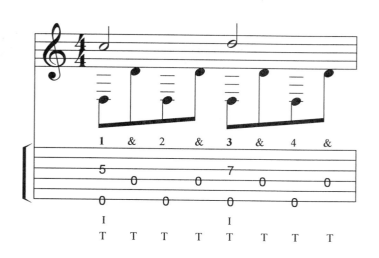

169

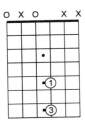

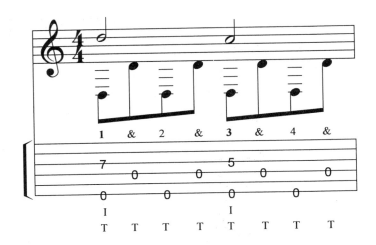

Now we play on all four beats.

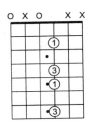

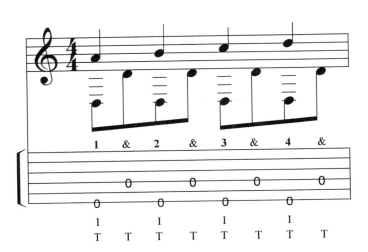

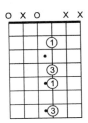

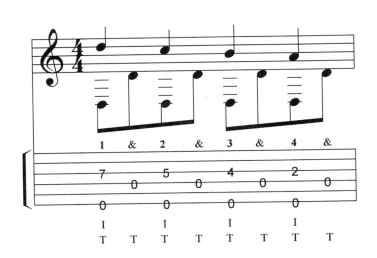

170

LEARNING THE UPBEATS

These are the upbeats of the 1 beat.

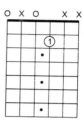

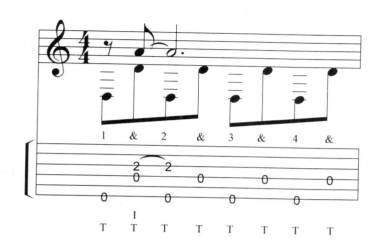

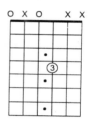

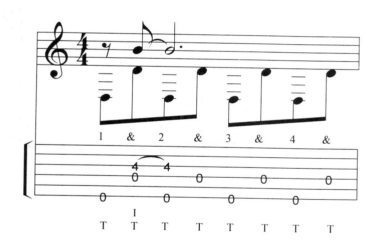

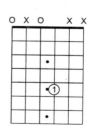

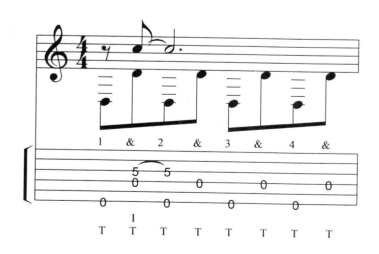

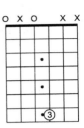

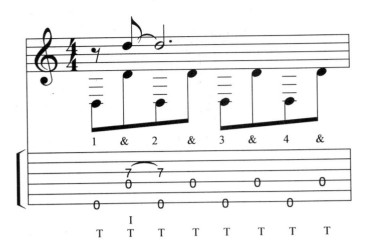

These are the upbeats of the 2 beat.

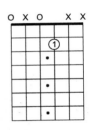

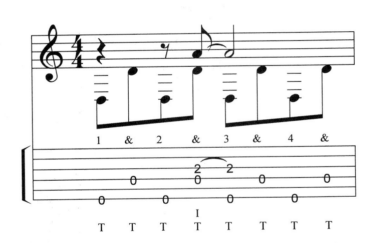

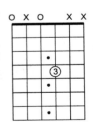

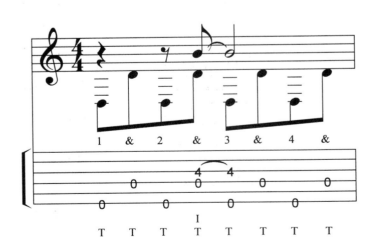

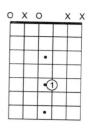

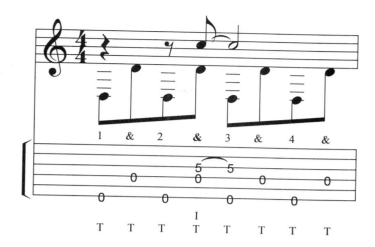

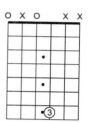

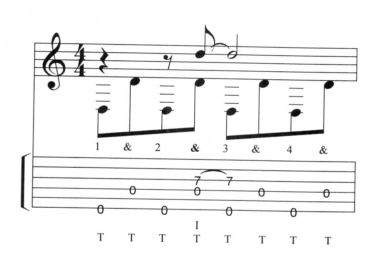

These are the upbeats of the 3 beat.

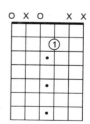

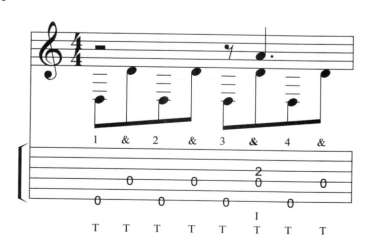

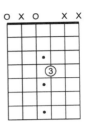

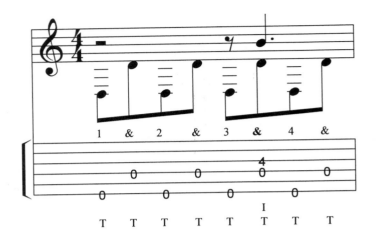

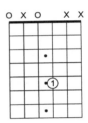

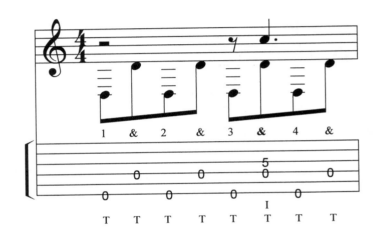

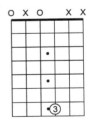

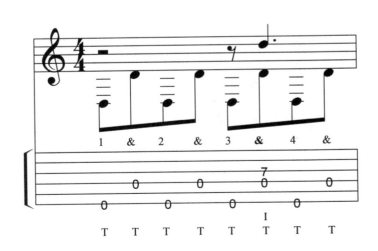

These are the upbeats of the 4 beat.

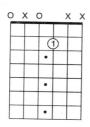

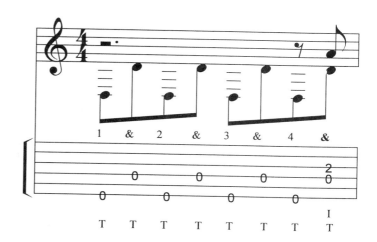

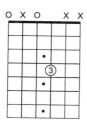

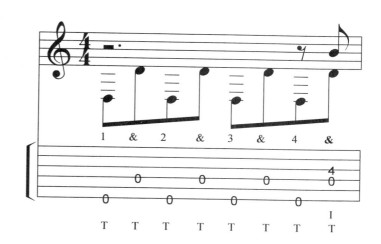

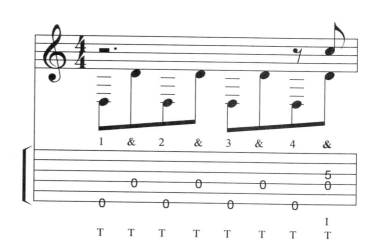

175

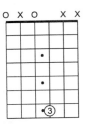

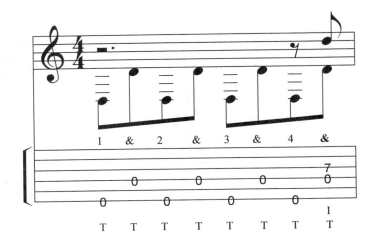

Two notes on the upbeats in a measure over the ostinato.

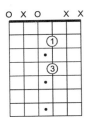

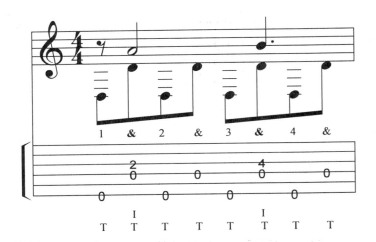

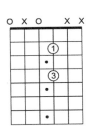

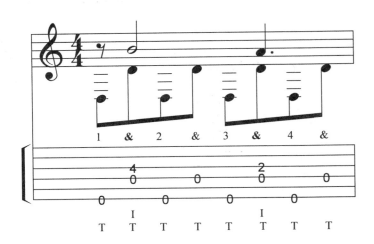

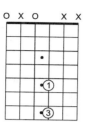

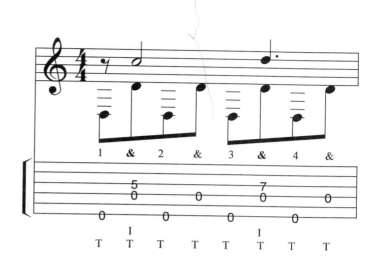

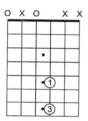

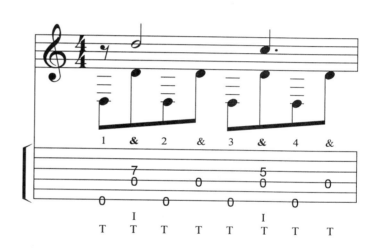

All of the upbeats in a measure.

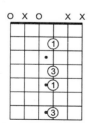

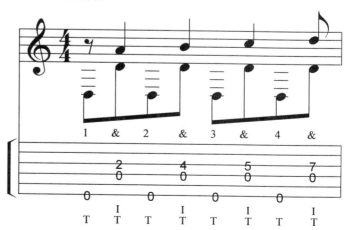

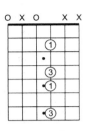

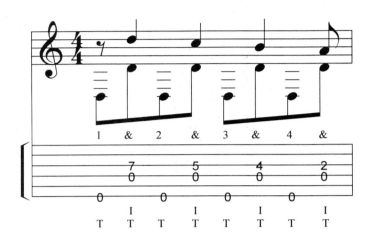

MIXING THE DOWN AND UPBEATS

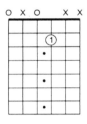

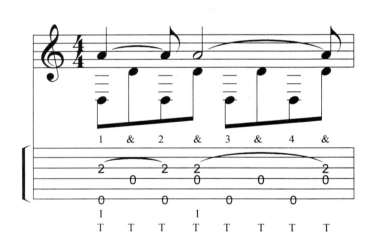

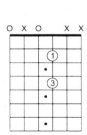

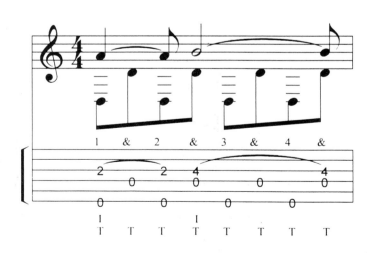

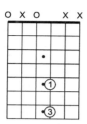

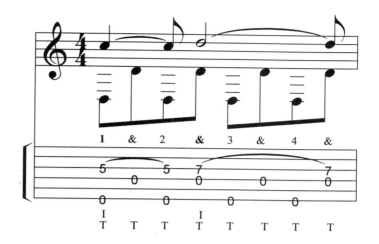

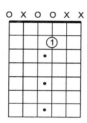

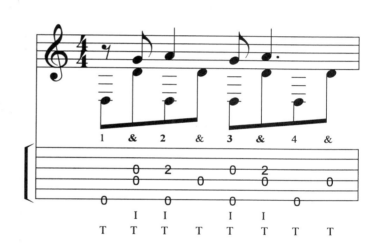

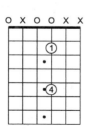

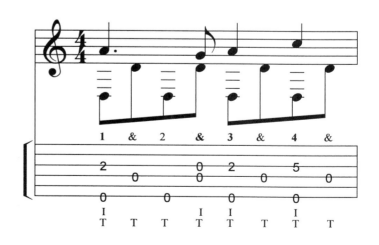

179

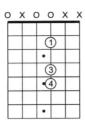

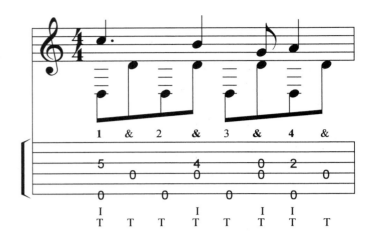

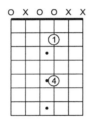

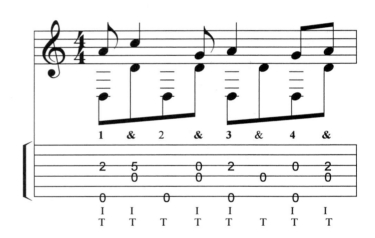

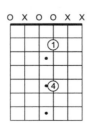

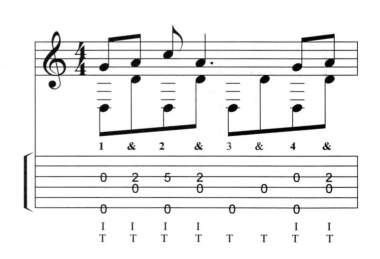

180

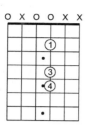

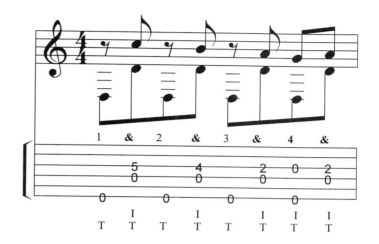

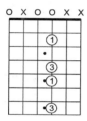

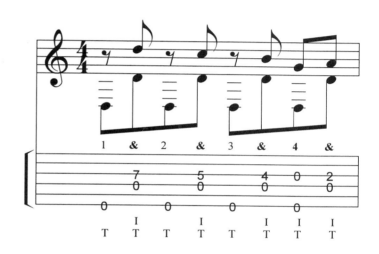

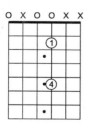

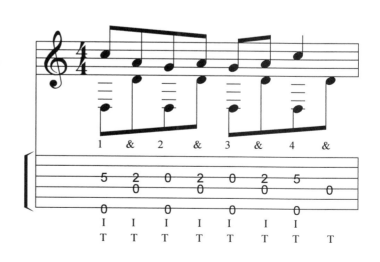

181

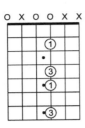
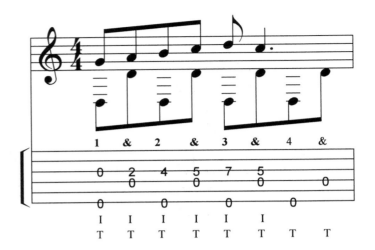

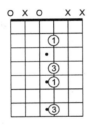
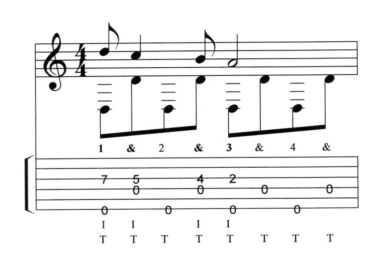

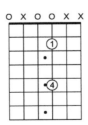
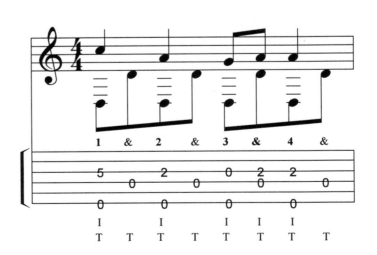

INTRODUCING NEW NOTES ON THE THIRD STRING

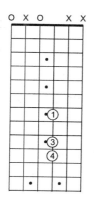

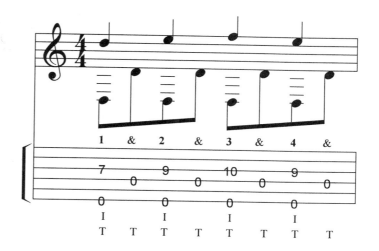

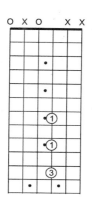

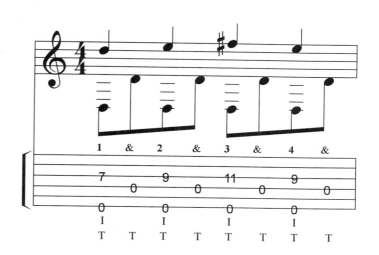

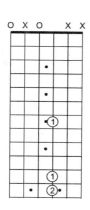

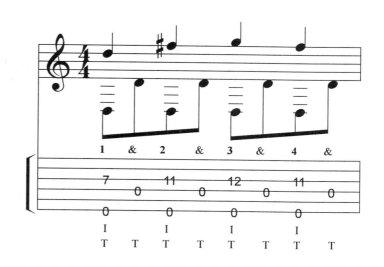

183

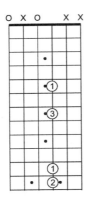

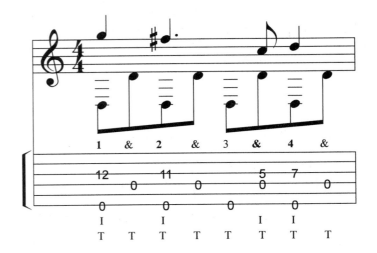

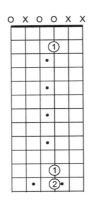

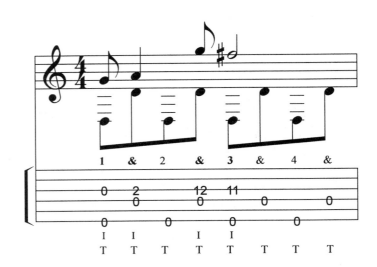

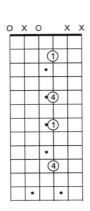

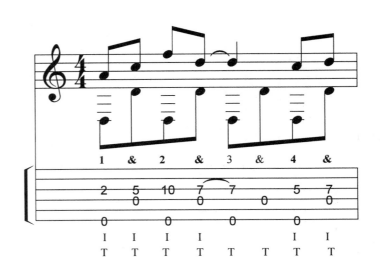

184

Any of the patterns you have learned thus far can be combined to create two measure patterns that repeat. Start toying around with that. These next two pages have examples of paired patterns that you have learned to give you an idea of what I mean. Some of the patterns have been altered only from D major to D minor.

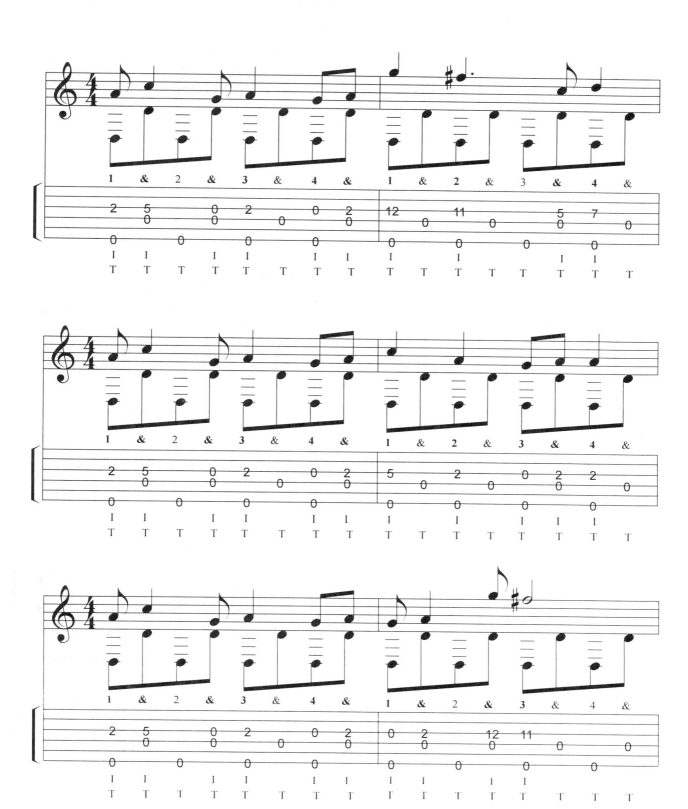

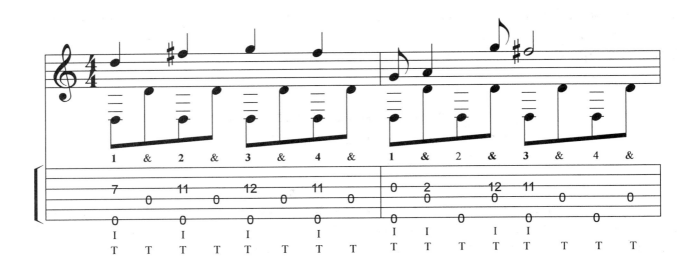

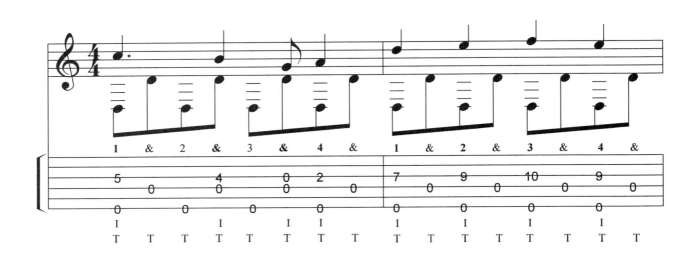

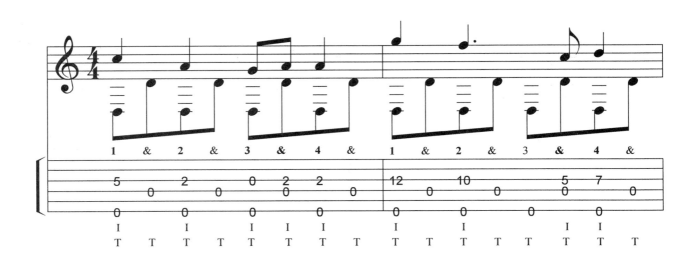

INTRODUCING SIXTEENTH NOTES

When you counted the eighths, you counted out 1 & 2 & 3 & 4 &. The 1, 2, 3, 4 being the down beats and the &'s being the up beats. When you use sixteenth notes you add beats between the down and up beats. You do that by counting 1 e & a, 2 e & a, 3 e & a, 4 e & a. The "a" is pronounced like up, or cup.

1 e & a 2 e & a 3 a & a 4 e & a

Now let's start one sixteenth at a time over the open D ostinato bass just like we did with the eighth notes. The left and right hand fingerings are the same as everything we did with the eighths, except for the fact that we are playing notes in between the up and down beats, the down beats being the low D and the up beats being the higher D.

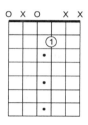

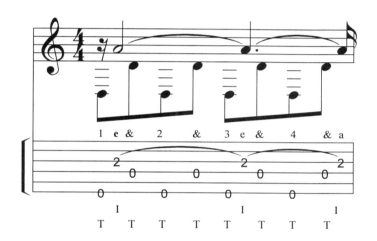

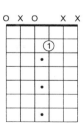

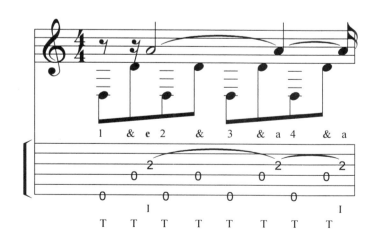

187

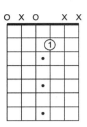
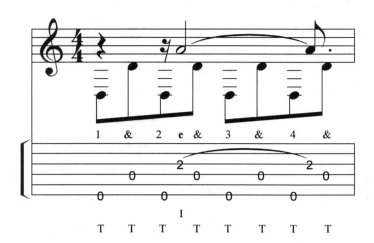

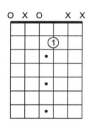
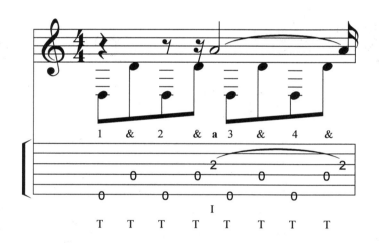

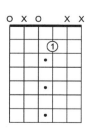
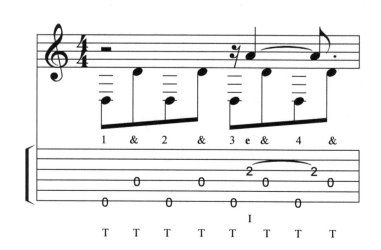

188

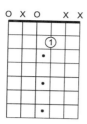

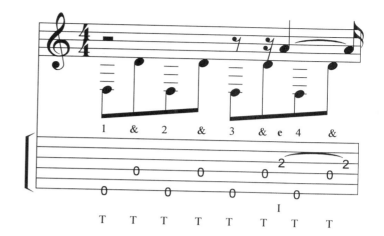

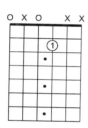

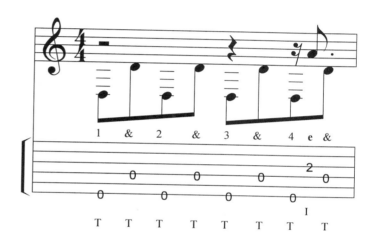

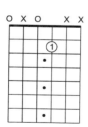

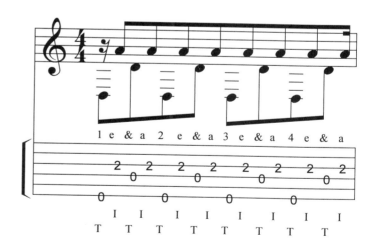

189

MIXING THE EIGHTHS AND SIXTEENTHS

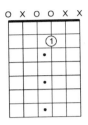

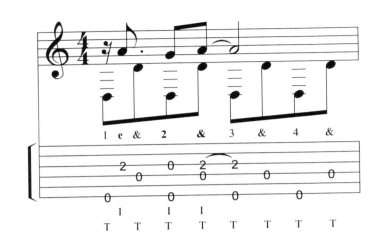

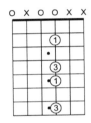

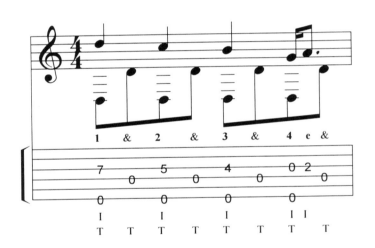

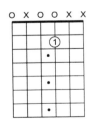

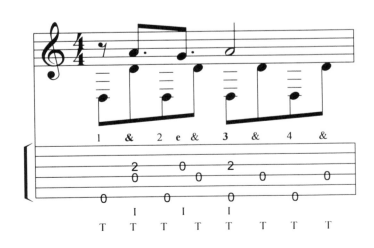

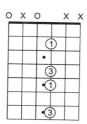

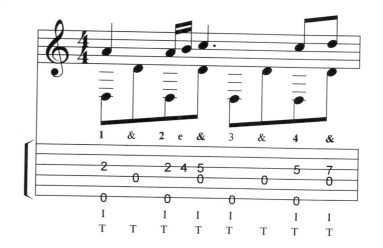

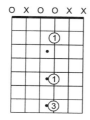

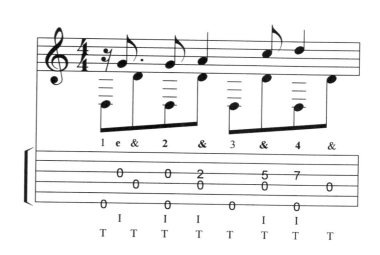

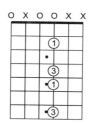

191

USING THE SECOND STRING WITH OSTINATO BASS

We're not going to spend as much time on the second and first string because you can apply everything that you learned so far on the third string to the second and first strings.

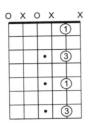

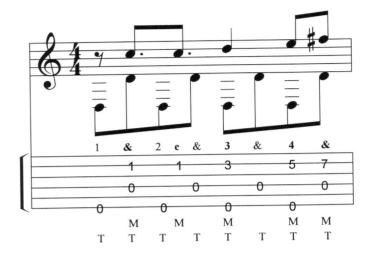

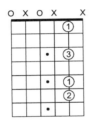

Same pattern done for D minor (note the F instead of F♯)

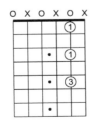

192

These are all the notes on the second string. Use the rhythms you learned from the third string and make up your own patterns with these notes.

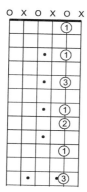

Play an F instead of F♯ for a D minor

USING THE FIRST STRING WITH OSTINATO BASS

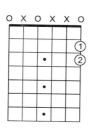

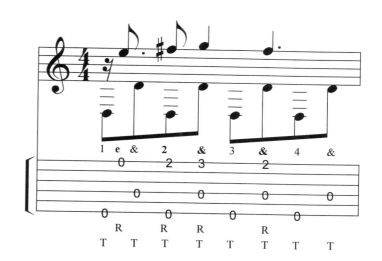

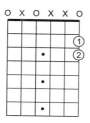

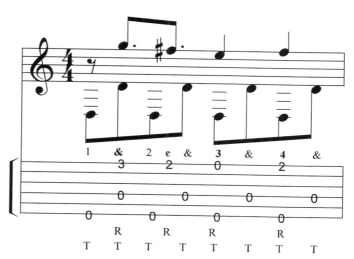

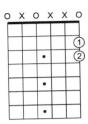

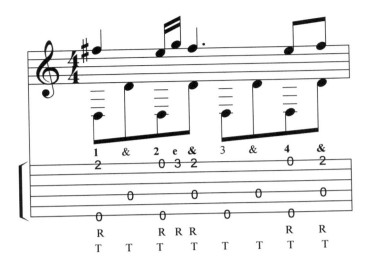

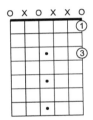

Same pattern done for D minor (note the F instead of F♯)

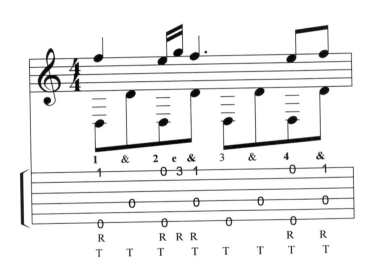

These are all the notes on the first string. Use the rhythms you learned from the third string and make up your own patterns.

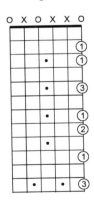

Play an F instead of F♯ for a D minor

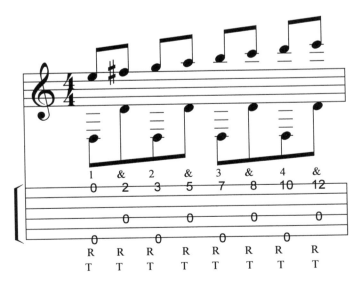

194

MIXING THE STRINGS

Now we start playing more than one string at a time while doing the ostinato bass. Start at a slow speed and gradually increase speed as you progress. We'll start by using the third and second string.

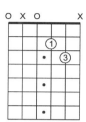

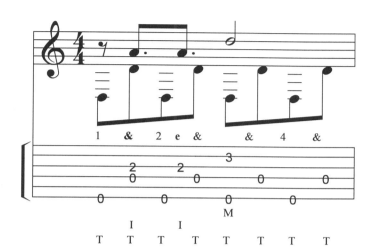

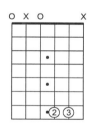

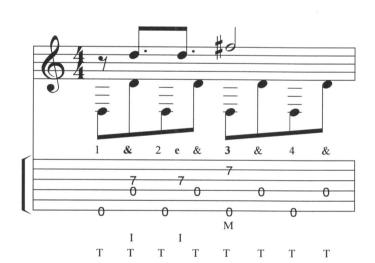

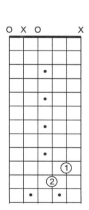

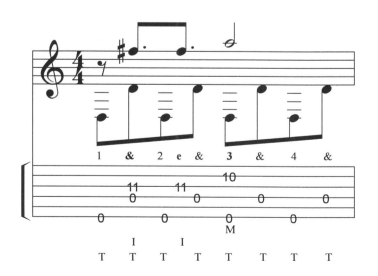

195

The notes in the fingering diagrams for the chord patterns represent all the notes being used in the measure and the L.H. fingering for those notes. Work hand in hand with them and the info in the notation and TAB measure.

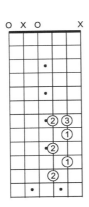

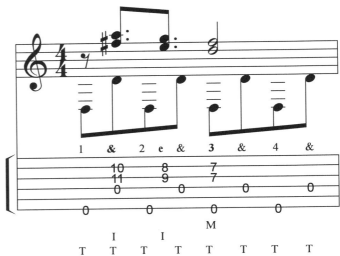

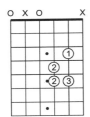 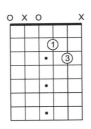

Because the fingering changes on the D note of the second string, this example required two diagrams.

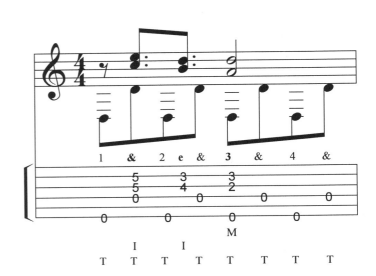

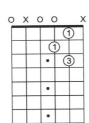

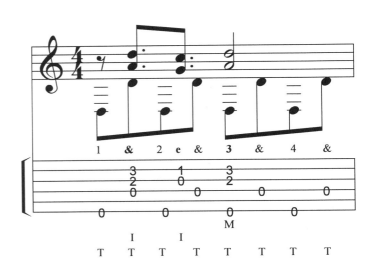

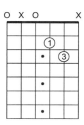

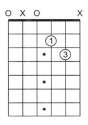

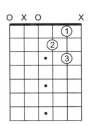

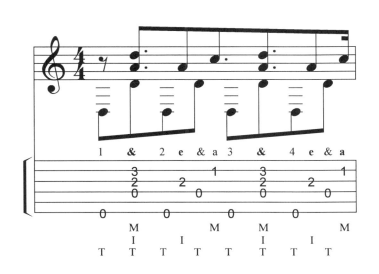

197

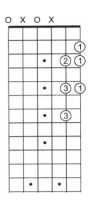
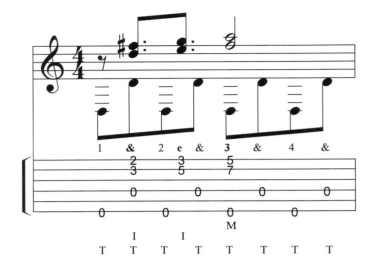

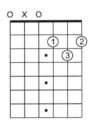
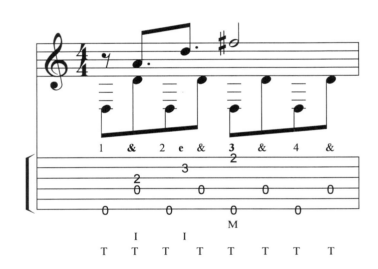

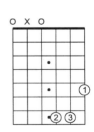
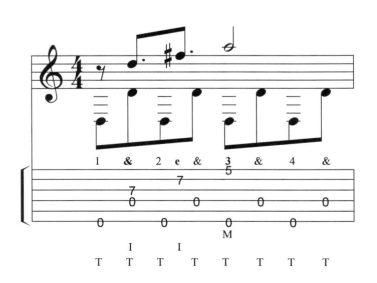

198

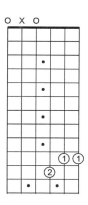

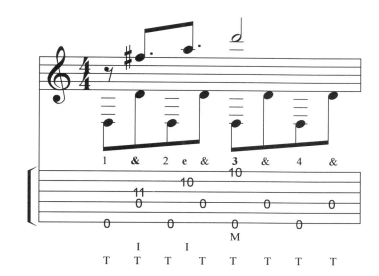

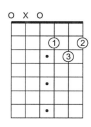

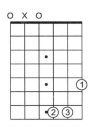

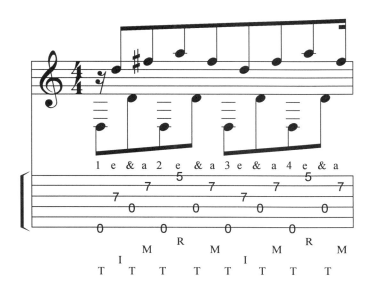

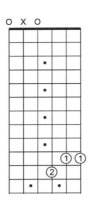

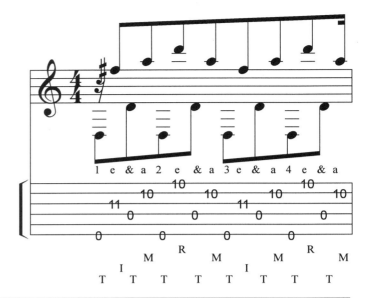

PLAYING OTHER CHORDS WHILE IN DROP D TUNING

You can change chords and still retain the ostinato bass. I prefer to use the thumb on the sixth string for this as it allows my little finger to do other things.

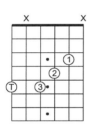

G

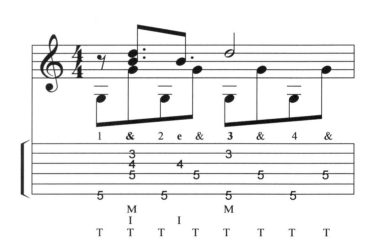

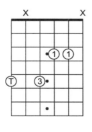

G⁻

(Gm)

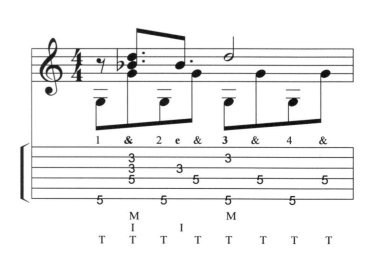

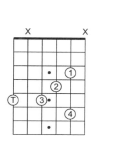

G7

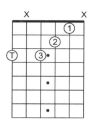

F

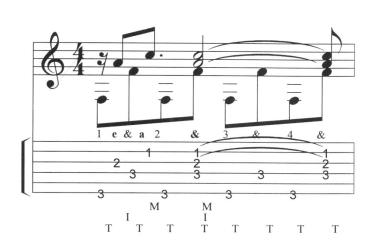

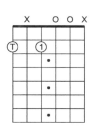

E⁻

(Em)

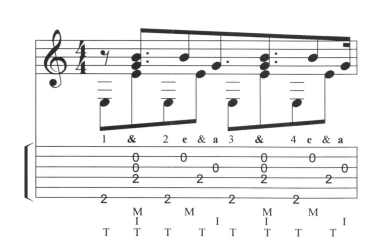

201

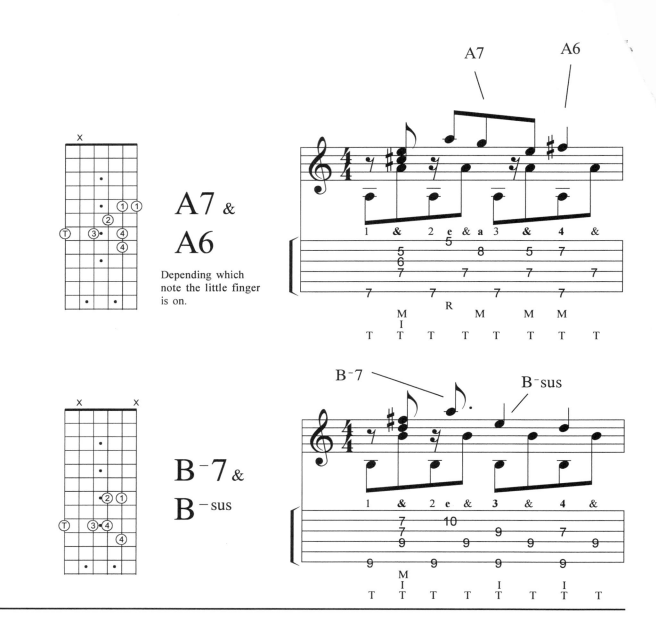

A7 &
A6

Depending which
note the little finger
is on.

B⁻7 &
B⁻sus

D MAJOR SCALE OVER OPEN D OSTINATO BASS

This one is a real toughy. Just take your time. It will help your fingerpicking all around. Hope you enjoyed this book.

ASCEND TO A HIGHER PLANE

GRIMOIRE®

BY ADAM KADMON

THE EXERCISE BOOK

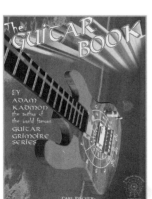

The Exercise Book offers players a fresh and disciplined approach to attaining mastery of the guitar. Laying out the entire foundation for developing dexterity on the guitar, it includes such unique features as 3 and 4 note scales and chordal "coils" for Major and Minor Pentatonic scales, picking patterns and diagrams for each of the "coils," connection of fingering patterns up and down the fretboard and special exercises designed to strengthen playing capacity. The Exercise Book is a thorough and complete compendium of exercises for the guitar.

GT100

THE QUICK CHORD BOOK

With this book Adam Kadmon has created a concise compendium of the basic guitar chords that are most often used by players in all styles, at all levels of performing ability. This book, designed for the novice guitarist, will show beginning players the essential chords quickly and facilitate mastery of a basic repertoire of chords in minutes. Each key is represented by 75 different chords from major and minor chords to thirteenth chords, shown in both fretboard position diagrams and traditional staff notation.

GT102

THE FINGERPICKING BOOK

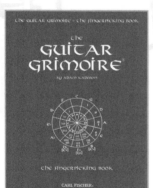

Starting with basic fingerpicking chord patterns and expanding to major and minor scales and bass ostinato variations, this book uses thousands of fingerboard diagrams, charts and musical examples (conventional staff and tablature) to guide and instruct players in the best way to master the techniques of playing finger-picking guitar and enhance their playing facility. Practical applications are suggested to make use of the material in the creation of original songs and compositions.

GT103

THE RHYTHM GUITAR BOOK

This is a path-breaking new book for a usually overlooked aspect of guitar playing: the special techniques needed for mastering the playing of rhythm guitar. Utilizing his renowned approach to music and the guitar, Kadmon explains and illustrates rhythm, intervals, chord riffs, finger picking and covers much more essential material that rhythm guitarists need to know.

GT104

THE GUITAR BOOK

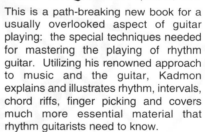

Drawing on the material he created for the *Guitar Grimoire®*, Adam Kadmon has put together a book that concentrates on the essential material guitarist's need in order to attain mastery of the musical use of the instrument. *The Guitar Book* contains sections on scales, modes, chords, progressions, solo techniques, theory and analysis and other vital topics derived from the highly successful Grimoire folios.

GT101

THE GUITARIST'S KEYBOARD PROGRESSIONS BOOK

With the use of MIDI & Computers, Guitarists today need to become proficient keyboard players. This book offers the guitarist a deeper understanding of Music Theory through keyboard study. Kadmon applies his results-oriented approach by teaching chord progressions and harmony at the keyboard.

In a visually clear format, the book covers chord theory, variations in voicing, a full survey of four-measure progressions and many other approaches to designing individual progressions that will enhance the performer's ability to perform and create.

GT105

- Learn to play any scale in any key on your fret board
- Perfect visual guide to the *Guitar Grimoire* Scales & Modes book
- Pop-up chords and fretboard close-ups

DVD2 – Scales & Modes

- Wizard-like details on how to play *any* chord imaginable
- Perfect guide to the *Guitar Grimoire – Chords & Voicings* book
- Includes polychords, chord substitutions, inversions and movable voicings

DVD3 – Chords & Voicings

- Learn how standard progressions are created and how to create your own
- Perfect guide to the *Guitar Grimoire Progressions & Improvisation* book
- Learn how to enhance & enrich your solos

DVD4 – Progressions & Improvisation

◆◆ *Approximate running time 60 minutes each*

The WIZARD SPEAKS!
— On DVD —

AT LONG LAST, THE WIZARD REVEALS, IN PERSON, THE MYSTERIES OF PLAYING THE GUITAR.

This all-new DVD series offers guitar students the opportunity to see and hear Adam Kadmon reveal and demonstrate the techniques and understanding of the underlying structure of music that have helped make the books of *The Guitar Grimoire* among the best-selling guitar teaching publications of all time.

Don't forget these exciting GUITAR GRIMOIRE® titles which correspond to the new DVDs

Scales & Modes (Bk.1)
GT1

Chords & Voicings (Bk.2)
GT2

Progressions & Improvisation (Bk.3)
GT15